CANALS IN WALES

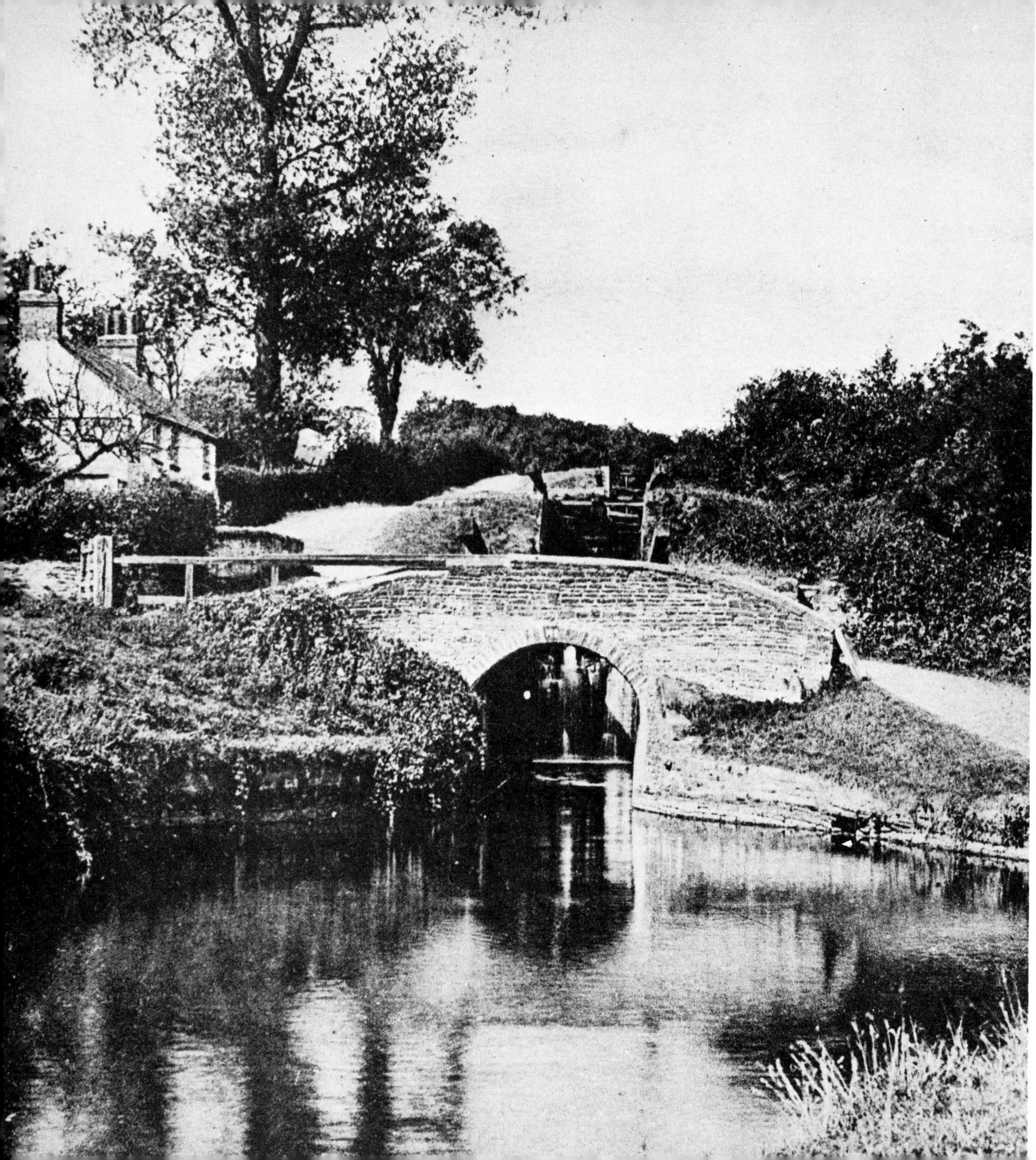

CANALS IN WALES

IAN L. WRIGHT

D. BRADFORD BARTON LIMITED

Frontispiece: The Monmouthshire Canal's impressive Fourteen Locks at Cefn, near Newport, engineered by Thomas Dadford, junior. The Crumlin Arm rose 178′ in under ¾ mile to reach the Ebbw Valley high above Rogerstone. This photograph, taken about 1900, shows a passing place about a third of the way up the flight. The bridge is a roving bridge carrying the towpath from one side of the canal to the other. [W. Hamlin Collection]

© copyright D. Bradford Barton 1977   774/2 NB   ISBN 0 85153 314 0

printed in Great Britain by H. E. Warne Ltd, London and St. Austell

for the publishers

D. BRADFORD BARTON LTD · Trethellan House · Truro · Cornwall · England

introduction

This book is the first to illustrate in photographs all the canals of Wales. It was in South Wales that my love for them developed. The Glamorganshire Canal, passing less than a mile from my home in Cardiff, was only just alive when I began exploring it in 1943. The collapse of a bank at Nantgarw the previous year had put an end to the carrying traffic, and it was the lucky combination of a new box Brownie camera and the unexpected appearance of Harry Watts shafting a boat at Llandaff, that resulted in the only live photographs of the canal I ever took.

I have been discovering canals with boat and camera ever since, nourished on L.T.C. Rolt's evocative 'Narrow Boat' and on the beautiful photographs of Eric de Maré taken on a now-famous cruise from London to Llangollen in 1948. I bought CHESWARDINE, a 17-foot canoe, joined the Inland Waterways Association, and set out to explore all the South Wales waterways that still had water in them. 1949 was a vintage year. I crossed the aqueducts over the Neath, cruised by Neath Abbey, and portaged my way from Newport to Brecon. Maybe in the May of that year I became the last-ever voyager up the Swansea Canal, then still intact between Morriston and Ystradgynlais. Out of these adventures of twenty-seven years ago comes much of the first hand material in this book.

My purpose is to provide the first visual record of all the canals in Wales, and of some of the people whose working lives were bound up with them. Much of the material is historical for, sadly, many miles are derelict and some, like the Swansea and the Glamorganshire, have disappeared for ever as new roads, housing developments, and industries have obliterated them. Even on the Welsh canals that survive, the way of life of the boatman had vanished shortly after the outbreak of the second World War. Compiling this survey has been a fascinating but difficult task, for the amount of picture material in libraries and collections is unbelievably scanty. There are thousands of photographs celebrating the drama and power of the steam railway in Wales, but few photographs seem to have recorded the quiet and hidden world of her canals.

Though there were a few blighted spots of industrial squalor on the South Wales canals—notably in the lower Swansea Valley—the visual contribution to Welsh landscape was rich indeed. Long ribbons of silver enlivened the view, whitewashed lock cottages joined the Welsh farmhouse in the landscape, and locks and weirs bubbled with water, whilst the high and winding contours around hill slopes soon grew into the landscape to provide homes for wild creatures. At the beginning of the 19th century, travellers like Malkin, riding through Wales in search of the picturesque, found the canals too straight, but commented on their structures, locks, and aqueducts as objects of wonder. Near Ruabon and Chirk on the Ellesmere Canal, the great works of Jessop and Telford survive today as engineering marvels in stone and iron. In South Wales the discovery of an industrial and transport heritage has come almost too late. The Swansea & Mumbles Railway disappeared as recently as 1960, whilst at Abercynon—scene of Trevithick's pioneer steam-hauled passenger journey of 1804—one looks in vain for the Penydarren Tramroad, the Basin, or the Glamorganshire Canal's great lock staircase.

During the Canal Age, 205 miles of waterway were constructed in Wales, a total of 41 miles within the old counties of Denbigh, Flint, and Montgomery, and 164 miles within Glamorgan, Monmouth, Brecon, and Carmarthen. Those in the north eventually became a unified system of railway-controlled canals forming the Welsh section of the Shropshire Union Railways & Canal Co. The Welsh Section lay partly within England and partly in Wales and its administrative hub was Ellesmere. Now generally called the Llangollen Canal, the section now open leaves the S.U. main line at Hurleston near Nantwich and enters Wales briefly at Bettisfield and finally at Chirk, where it continues its spectacular journey to Llangollen. The long disused Newtown Arm left the Llangollen line at Welsh Frankton and crossed the Welsh border at Llanymynech. It formed part of the old Ellesmere system as far as Carreghofa; then, as the Montgomeryshire Canal, it struck across country to the Severn which it followed through Welshpool to Newtown. The S.U. system was a narrow canal network with locks capable of passing boats 70' by 6' 10".

By contrast, South Wales presented a fragmented group of relatively short canals conceived in isolation from one another and from the rest of the British canal network. They followed narrow river valleys, were heavily locked, and were built to varying lock and boat dimensions. Places out of reach of the canals were connected to them by extensive systems of tramroads. The greatest of the South Wales waterways, the Glamorganshire, obtained its act in 1790 and triggered off the building of 77 miles of canals within the years 1794-1799. The Glamorgan, the Neath, the Monmouthshire, and the Swansea were all completed during this period, engineered almost entirely by Thomas Dadford, Thomas Sheasby, and their sons. The Aberdare, the Brecon & Abergavenny, the Kidwelly & Llanelly, and the Tennant were other major canals completed after 1800.

In Wales the canals greatly accelerated the progress of the Industrial Revolution, particularly in the south where they clung precariously to the sides of the narrow valleys of the Taff, Tawe, Ebbw, and Usk, bringing iron and coal for export at the developing river ports of Newport, Cardiff, and Swansea. Nor was their importance purely local, for the Glamorganshire carried the iron cannon that helped to defeat Napoleon and was the means of introducing London to Merthyr steam coal. The Ellesmere and the Montgomeryshire played their part in the Napoleonic struggle by assisting home agriculture: they carried stone and coal to rural limekilns that were producing lime for rough hill pastures ploughed up to support corn. From the 1850's the canals of Wales lost their dominance to the railways, but continued to be useful for another thirty years. Unable to compete, the canals were carrying little traffic by 1900, and they survived into the twentieth century as suppliers of water to industry rather than as important arteries of transport. For reasons physical and economic, the canals of North and South Wales never met, and, because of their differences in character, I have treated them separately within this survey.

The Welsh canals were almost unknown in 1950. Today there are 45 miles open for recreation and amenity. Restoration owes much to the Inland Waterways Association whose first South Wales campaign at Brecon in 1952 persuaded the British Transport Commission to give up plans to abandon the Brecon Canal and changed the official attitude of county councils wanting to lower or pipe the canal's principal road bridges. The Shropshire Union Canal Society, the Newport Canal Society, and the Neath & Tennant Canal Society are among voluntary organisations dedicated to waterway restoration in Wales today, and undoubtedly the most exciting project for many years is the Prince of Wales Committee's adoption of a scheme to restore seven miles of the Montgomeryshire Canal with the financial support of the Variety Club of Great Britain. My sincere thanks are due to the many people who have granted me the use of their copyright and assisted in my research work for this book. I am especially grateful to Messrs. Harry Arnold, Charles Hadfield, W. Hamlin, R. Hutchings, A. Lewery, G. Rattenbury, D. Morgan Rees, and E. Paget-Tomlinson for their help, and to many past friends among boatmen and canal workers whose treasures of canal lore have thrown light on a little-known aspect of Welsh social history.

Northampton   Ian L. Wright

Acknowledgements accompany each illustration except
in the case of the author's own work.

The Sea Lock of the Glamorganshire Canal at Cardiff in 1891. The canal was extended to the Sea Lock in 1798 and vessels up to 200 tons could be admitted to a mile-long floating harbour. *Elizabeth Ann* of Porlock is seen here discharging flour at the Sea Lock Basin.
[County of South Glamorgan Libraries: Cardiff]

GLAMORGANSHIRE CANAL

The Glamorganshire Canal was the promotion of Merthyr ironmasters, the Crawshays of Cyfarthfa, the Homfrays of Penydarren, the Hills of Plymouth works, and the Guests of Dowlais, all anxious for improved transport down the Taff Valley to the Bristol Channel seaboard at Cardiff for the export of manufactured iron. The Act of 1790 authorised a canal 24½ miles long from Merthyr to Cardiff. There were originally 50 locks with a total fall of 543 feet, the engineer-contractors being Thomas Dadford, his son, also Thomas, and Thomas Sheasby. The canal was opened for traffic in 1794, and extended to a sea lock in 1798. Rapid growth in the iron industry followed and in 1830 over 201,000 tons of iron and coal were carried. In 1851 the total tonnage from all classes of traffic had reached over 581,000, in spite of ten years of competition from the Taff Vale Railway. However, by 1870 tonnages had dropped dramatically, as the railways, with their better dock handling facilities, took away most of the canal's business. Moreover, mining subsidence closed the Merthyr section in 1898 and the Abercynon—Pontypridd portion in 1915, whilst the remaining Cardiff—Pontypridd portion saw its last boat in 1942. Cardiff Corporation bought the canal in 1944 and the property was developed for other purposes, but a short section of the Sea Lock pound remained in use until 1951.

The Sea Lock Basin, Cardiff, in 1950. Sandridge & Co's *Catherine Ethel* and J & R Griffiths' *Britannia* are seen at the sand wharves adjoining Harrowby Street in Cardiff's dockland, after discharging sea-dredged sand from the Bristol Channel. Behind them is the New Sea Lock Hotel. This last-surviving half mile section of the Glamorganshire Canal, now transformed into one of the city's parks, came to a dramatic end on 5 December 1951 when *Catherine Ethel* hit the Sea Lock gates, emptied the Sea Lock pound, and was carried out to sea in the flood of water.

A canal street name in Butetown, Cardiff.
[W. Hamlin]

East and West Wharves of the Glamorganshire Canal, seen from the lower end of St. Mary Street, Cardiff, about 1905, looking towards Butetown and the sea. Indicating the former maritime importance of the canal is the Custom House, on the corner site behind the electric tram. Beyond the G.W.R. South Wales main line railway bridge are the Canal Company's Wharf, office and railway. The moored boats at East Canal Wharf are Star, Crown, and Anchor patent fuel works boats awaiting horse towing to Blackweir and Maindy after delivering cargoes to shipping in the Bute Docks via the connecting Junction Canal. [W. Hamlin Collection]

West Wharf, Cardiff, about 1890, with a Bridgwater ketch and Glamorgan Canal Co's boat No. 491 lying at T. G. Williams' wharf, the upper limit of navigation for sea-going vessels. The ketch has probably brought in a consignment of bricks, tiles, and pipes from Bridgwater on the River Parrett. The builders' merchants still trade from a nearby site, but the canal has been covered by industrial development.

[W. Hamlin Collection]

Glamorganshire Canal Railway locomotive shunting at Clarence Road level crossing in 1957. Authorised in 1882, the railway served wharves and warehouses along the west side of the canal from West Canal Wharf to the Sea Lock, and was connected to the G.W.R. Riverside Branch by a level crossing over Dumballs Road. The railway became the property of Cardiff Corporation in 1944 and its last steam locomotive *Delwyn* was replaced in 1947 by the Greenwood & Batley battery-electric shunter seen in this photograph, with the City of Cardiff coat-of-arms on its cab side. The railway was worked at a loss for many years but was not closed until 1963. Beyond the crossing may be seen the James Street Swing Bridge which still spanned the dry bed of the canal in 1957.

Mill Lane, Cardiff, about 1936, showing St. Mary Street and Penarth Road, with the Glamorganshire Canal separated by a stone wall. Custom House Bridge spanned the canal on the extreme left. Until about 1949, when it was filled in to accommodate road alterations and a street market, the canal followed the course of Cardiff's medieval wall and Town Ditch.
[H. B. Priestley]

A boat approaches North Gate Bridge, Cardiff, near the Castle and present day Kingsway, on its way through the town to the docks. From an engraving of about 1880.
[W. Hamlin Collection]

Mynachdy Lock, the 48th from Cyfarthfa, managing to preserve a rural atmosphere in this photograph of 1947, taken within two miles of Cardiff's city centre. The Canal Company followed the traditional Welsh custom of limewashing its cottages and lock houses.

Tom Fraser leads his horse out of Crockherbtown Lock, Cardiff, with a Canal Company's boat loaded with flour for the Hopkin Morgan Basin, Pontypridd, about 1936. An old weighing dock and weigh house survive to the right of the lock. Queen Street runs behind the building in the background where the canal emerges from The Tunnel, and another Cardiff street, The Friary, is beyond the boundary wall on the left.
[W. Hamlin Collection]

The 115 yard Tunnel under Queen Street, Cardiff, as it was in 1944. There was a short towpath at the northern end and boat horses were led up a paved horse way to street level and across the top of the tunnel between Queen Street and Hills Terrace. Meanwhile boatmen manhandled their boats through by grasping the chain fixed to the tunnel wall. The lane used by the horses had an official Cardiff street name—The Tunnel—and the whole site is today incorporated into the premises of Mackross Ltd.

A Glamorganshire Canal Co's boat lying in the dock of the Weighing Machine, North Road, Cardiff, in 1948. Built by Brown Lenox of Pontypridd in 1836, this cast-iron structure could weigh a boat and its cargo up to a limit of 40 tons. It was dismantled in 1955 and reassembled at the Waterways Museum, Stoke Bruerne, Northamptonshire, in 1963.

Glamorganshire Canal Co's boat No. 451 on maintenance duties near Llandaff North, 1943. South Wales canal boats were utilitarian craft, not greatly admired for the beauty of their lines. Ancestors were almost certainly the early straight-sided narrow boats designed by James Brindley for the Duke of Bridgewater's underground colliery canals at Worsley. No. 451 was 60' long by 8' 9" beam and typical of most South Wales types, with a carrying capacity of 21 tons.

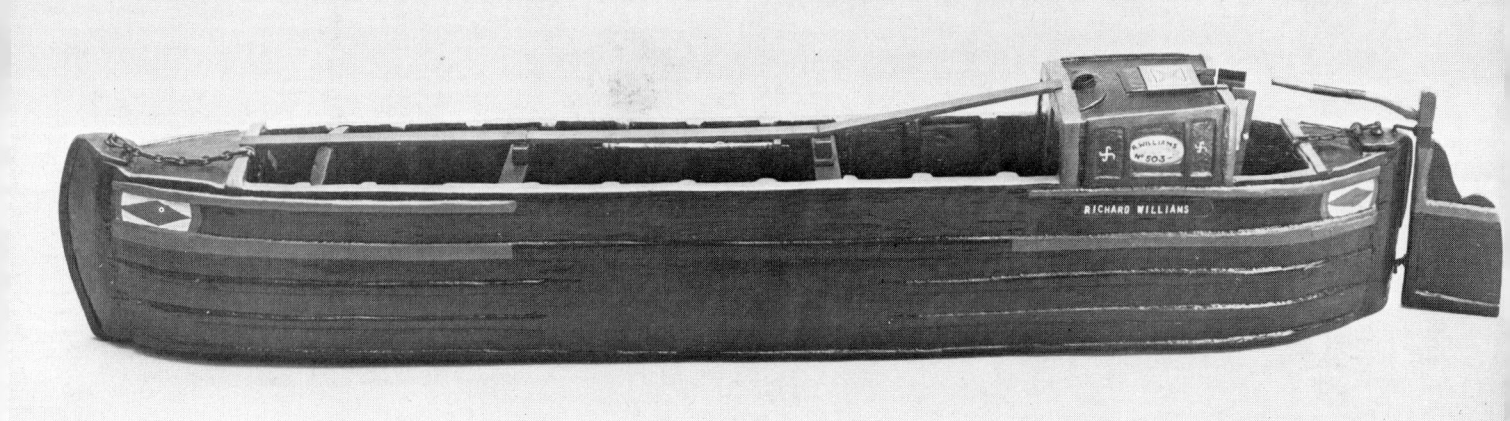

Bye trader's boat, about 1890. This model, built by canal boatman Richard Williams, Senior, of Rhydyfelin, about 85 years ago, was discovered by the author in 1949 and is now in the National Museum of Wales. The 'lozenge and crescent' bow and stern plates and 'four pears' designs on the cabin are rare survivals of a South Wales tradition in boat decoration. [National Museum of Wales]

Welsh boat horse, 1906. Tom Fraser, as a boy of sixteen, poses with his horse at Treble Locks near Taff's Well, in the summer of 1906. In common with all South Wales boatmen, Fraser lived 'ashore' in a canal bank cottage with no tradition of family life on the boats. The South Wales boat was worked by a man and a boy, and apart from a interlude with steam haulage, the Glamorganshire Canal remained faithful to horse power for all its 148 years. Tom Fraser, and William Bladen of Llandaff North, became the last working boatmen in Wales when the Canal Company's Cardiff to Pontypridd goods traffic ended in 1942.
[W. Hamlin Collection]

Experiment in steam. Goods traffic on the Glamorganshire Canal entered a brief period of expansion when the Marquis of Bute took control of the company in 1885. The company itself began carrying in 1887 and in 1893 purchased the steel-built steam tug *Bute,* seen here at the Cambrian Yard maintenance depot at Gabalfa, Cardiff, about 1906. Built by Alsopp & Sons of Preston, *Bute* was the only steam tug on the canal. She carried 18 tons of cargo and towed three or four boats. Two trips were made between Cardiff and Pontypridd in 1893 but the experiment was not successful. It took too long to pass *Bute* and each of her boats separately through the fifteen narrow locks. Work was, however, found for her on the Cardiff end of the canal, and until withdrawal in 1914 she was active on the Melingriffith run, carrying tinplate for export at Cardiff Docks.

[W. Hamlin Collection]

Severe winters brought blockade by ice. The Company's ice breaker, manned by a crew of nine men and hauled by two horses, forces a channel through the ice at Mynachdy Cottages, near Western Avenue, Cardiff, in the winter of 1940-41. The crew broke up the ice by gripping the handrails and vigorously rocking the boat from side to side.

Melingriffith Pump, 1807. The Melingriffith Tinplate Works was one of a number of forges, mills, and works depending on the river Taff for water power, and in 1806 the owners, Harford Partridge & Co., took court action against the Canal Co. for diverting most of the Taff's water into the canal and thus bringing Melingriffith to a standstill during dry summers. One result of the dispute was this pump, erected in 1807 under the supervision of Rennie and Jessop, and operated by a 14½' diameter cast-iron water wheel in the works' tail race. Now the major Glamorganshire Canal relic, the pump with its 20' oak rocker beams was last in regular use in 1927, raising water out of the mill race and passing it into the canal at Melingriffith Lock. From 1809 the Canal Co. was also working a Boulton & Watt steam engine at Pontyryn, near Troedyrhiw, where water that had turned the wheels of Hill's Plymouth Iron Works was pumped back into the canal's Four Mile Pound.

The ice breaker awaiting its fate at the Cambrian Yard, Gabalfa, in 1947. The hull was built of oak and sheathed with iron plates.

John James, founder of the Gabalfa boat building business of John James & Son. Born in 1822, James emigrated to South Wales from Llanon, Cardiganshire, in the 1860's. In the 1880's there were three dry docks at James's boatyard, where a new boat could be turned out for £80 and, with a cabin, for £90. John Rees James, a son, took over the dock in 1908, when the sole remaining work was the repair of Star Patent Fuel Works boats and a small amount of hiring. The dock closed in 1927 when the patent fuel traffic ended.
[Author's Collection]

A Welsh canal boatyard; the Glamorganshire Canal Co's dry dock at Cambrian Yard, Gabalfa in December 1943, with boat No. 499 under repair. The site now forms part of Cardiff Corporation's Gabalfa housing estate.

GABALVA DOCK, *Llandaff,* 191

Letterheading of John James & Son, Gabalfa Dock, near Llandaff. [Author's Collection]

D^r to **JOHN JAMES & SON,**
BOAT BUILDERS AND OWNERS.

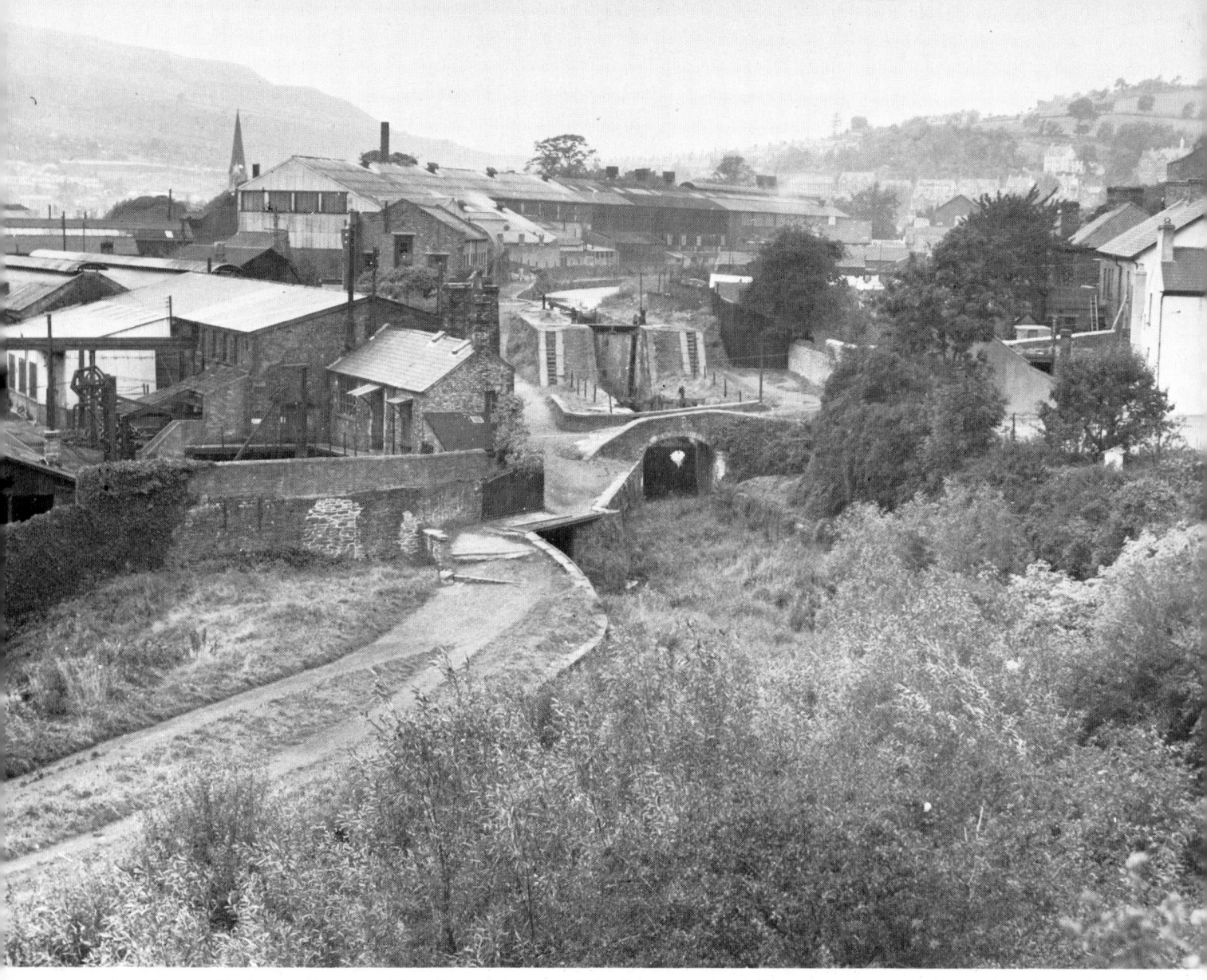

Canal-served industry, Pontypridd; a view of the east side of the town in 1949, showing the Glamorganshire Canal and the Brown Lenox Chain Works, established in 1816 for the manufacture of ships' anchors and cables. The firm made the chain for a number of early suspension bridges and chain piers and forged the cables for Brunel's *Great Eastern*. The raw materials—iron and coal from Aberdare and Merthyr—were boated into the upper works basin above the two Ynysangharad locks, and the finished cables were shipped out to Cardiff from the lower basin which remained in occasional use until 1939. Ynysangharad locks once provided a twenty foot head of water to drive the works machinery, augmented by supplies from the Berw feeder.

Newbridge Works, Pontypridd.

1060

13/6/ 1918

Permit Boat No. 302

B Gould Master

from Ynysyngharad to Cardiff

with Tons 16 Cwt

for BROWN LENOX & Co. Limited

A Brown Lenox loading bill of 1918. Ben Gould of Treforest, the last independent owner-boatman on the Glamorganshire Canal, was the regular Chain Works carrier.
[Author's Collection]

**PHILLIPS & MOGFORD,
PWLLGWAUN COLLIERY, PONTYPRIDD.**

29 July 1902

No. of Boat,
Name of Boatman B Gould
For Lewis Jenkins & Scale

Tons.	Cwts.	
15	10	LARGE COAL
		SMALL COAL
		THRO' & THRO' COAL

Doctor Griffiths' Canal. A loading bill for a consignment of coal by tramroad and canal, 1902. Pwllgwaun Colliery, a small pit in the lower Rhondda Valley, was still sending coal by Coffin's Tramroad for transhipment at the Treforest terminal of Dr. Griffiths' Canal as late as 1902. The boatman was Ben Gould. [Author's Collection]

The canal village of Nantgarw about 70 years ago, showing the canal wharf and the kilns and buildings of Nantgarw Pottery, producer of the world-famous porcelain between 1813 and 1822. The pottery site was chosen for its transport advantages, supplies of coal and imports of clay being sent by the Glamorganshire Canal. The pottery turned out stoneware, earthenware, and clay pipes until 1920 and sent much of its production by water.

[J. C. Pyper Collection]

The great Treble Locks at Taff's Well, in 1944, viewed from the top of the rise. Thomas Dadford engineered eleven sets of double locks on the upper reaches of the Glamorganshire Canal, a deep intermediate gate being common to both. This unique treble set gave a combined rise of 33' 8". The locks, which stood midway between Cardiff and Pontypridd, were destroyed in 1969 during the building of the Cardiff to Merthyr trunk road. Alongside the canal is the Rhiw Ddar reservoir, built about 1821.

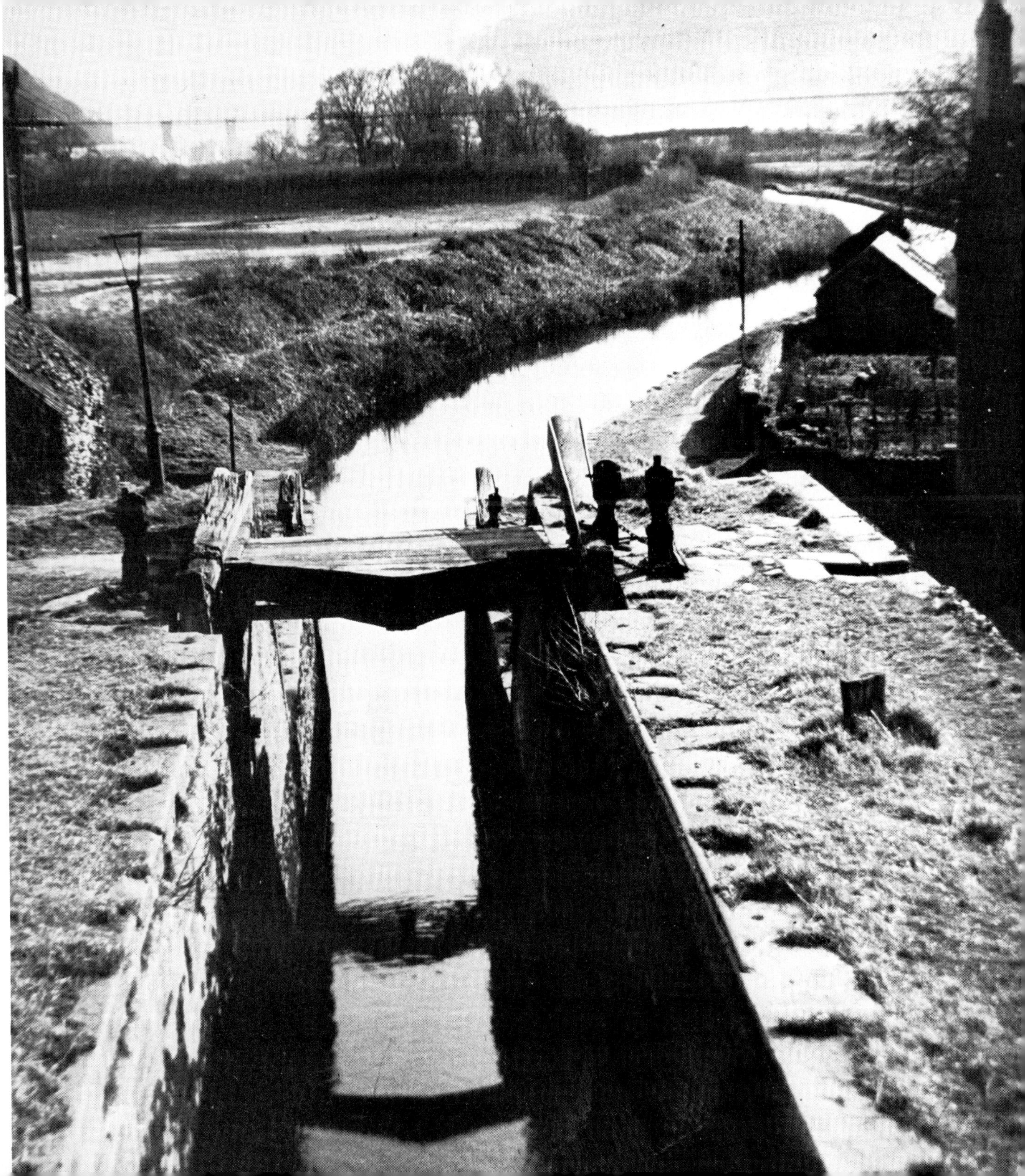

Ynysangharad Locks, Pontypridd, about 1936, with an empty G.C. Co goods boat preparing to leave for Cardiff. The boat's running planks will be noted, and the towline which has just been re-connected to the towing mast. The latter, which lies at an angle just behind the man in the boat, had to be inclined on an empty boat high in the water so as to ensure sufficient clearance under the canal's low bridges. The rare combination of canal engineering, architecture, and human interest in this photograph sum up all that is typical of the South Wales canal scene.

[Pontypridd Public Library]

Canal stoppage 1908; traffic held up at Foundry Bridge, Upper Boat, near Pontypridd, as a result of a breach in the canal at Dynea, in October 1908. The men are unloading one of the company's goods boats, No. 382, and transferring her cargo of provisions for the three mile road journey to Pontypridd. In the foreground is a clay boat assisting in the Dynea repair work.   [Pontypridd Public Library]

Bill Gomer of Rhydyfelin, 1950. In 1891, as a boy of nine, he started boating to Merthyr with his father on the boat *Rob Roy*. He worked at the Canal Co's Treforest warehouse until it closed in 1941 and in the 1950's, Cardiff Corporation employed him as a patrolman along the canal route south of Pontypridd.

Looking down the Abercynon lock staircase in 1913. This impressive engineering work, completed about 1792, was a concentration of sixteen locks in a distance of one mile, with a rise towards Merthyr of 207'. The locks seen here formed part of a group of eleven concentrated in only a quarter of a mile. To the left of the picture is the Canal Co's stonemasons' yard and the Quaker's Yard incline of the Taff Vale Railway. At the bottom of the flight a goods boat unloads in Lock Isaf. [Rowlands: Treforest]

Navigation House at Abercynon, dating from 1791, the administrative building of the Glamorganshire Canal Co. for almost a century, where the canal crossed the Taff by a stone aqueduct. It was the natural focus of routes from Merthyr, Aberdare, and Gelligaer, and the site of the Company's maintenance yard, sawpit, and dry dock. Navigation House became a public house about 1890 and is still open and little changed since canal days.

Trevithick's high pressure tram engine made its historic run on the Penydarren Tramroad from Merthyr to the basin at Navigation House (now Abercynon) on 21 February 1804. The first locomotive to run on rails, Trevithick's engine hauled five wagons, 70 men, and ten tons of bar iron over the 9¾ mile tramroad, and won a bet of £500 for Samuel Homfray, the Merthyr ironmaster.

The site of the Canal Head at Cyfarthfa, Merthyr Tydfil, as it was in 1947. This location, where water entered the canal from Crawshay's Cyfarthfa Works mill race, was 568' above sea level, and the highest level reached by a major canal in Wales. Remains of the ironworks are seen behind the bridge arch, which spanned the lines of the Cyfarthfa Works railway.

Quay Row, a canal name surviving in 1972 on cottages at Upper Abercanaid, where Robert and Lucy Thomas loaded the famous Waun Wyllt steam coal in the 1830's.

Lock No. 1 and the Canal Co's warehouse near Jackson's Bridge, Merthyr, in 1947. Beyond the lock is the site of the red ore wharf with its one-time tramroad connection to Ynysfach Works. The Cyfarthfa wagon shed, rail sheds, and boat repair yard are seen beyond, with Cyfarthfa Castle, the home of the Crawshays, on the hillside in the distance.

ABERDARE CANAL

This six-mile-long canal was authorised in 1793 but not opened until 1812. It ran from Aberdare to a junction with the Glamorganshire Canal at Abercynon, the engineers being Thomas Sheasby, Junior and George Overton. There were two locks. Iron, coal, pitwood, and limestone were the principal traffic, and an extensive system of tramroads linked the canal head with the ironworks at Abernant and Hirwaun, and with the Neath Canal at Glyn Neath. The Aberdare Canal came under the control of the Marquis of Bute in 1885 but had to be closed in 1900 because of mining subsidence in the Aberdare Valley. The canal has since disappeared almost without trace and most of its course has been covered by roads.

A rare photograph of a Welsh canal tramroad at work. The horses are hauling wagons loaded with limestone on the Aberdare Canal Co's Penderyn-Hirwaun tramroad about 1900. [Aberdare Public Library]

Aberdare Canal Junction in 1948, with the course of the Aberdare Canal branching left and the remains of the Glamorganshire Canal ascending through the ruined locks Nos. 17 and 16 towards Merthyr.

NEATH CANAL

The Neath Canal was 10½ miles long with 19 locks which could take boats about 60' long by 9' 0" beam and carrying up to 25 tons. It was built, under an Act of 1791, from Glyn Neath down the valley of the Neath river to Melincrythan Pill, below Neath, and was completed about 1795. Thomas Dadford, Junior superintended the lower section and Thomas Sheasby completed the rest of the line to Glyn Neath. The Neath Canal was extended to a better shipping place at Giant's Grave in 1799. The cargoes were coal, iron ore, limestone, silica, and gunpowder The canal became prosperous on coal, 200,000 tons annually being exported in the late 1850's. The Vale of Neath Railway (later the G.W.R.), had captured almost all the coal traffic by 1880, and by 1921 the canal was little used. The Neath Canal Navigation Co. still exists, and maintains the lower half of the canal for supplying water to industry, but parts of the canal course above Aberdulais may be incorporated into the route of the new Neath-Abergavenny Trunk road.

The Neath Canal Act of 1791 for 'making and maintaining' a canal from Abernant (Glyn Neath) to the Brickfield below the town of Neath.
[Alan Fowler]

In 1934 the Neath Canal Co. built at Tonna what must have been the last traditional wooden canal boat to be constructed in Wales. The boat was built by Ben Jones, the Company's foreman, seen at work on its construction in 1934. Named *Ivy May* after Jones's wife, the boat was still working on maintenance duties from Tonna in 1949. Last surviving example of a common South Wales type, *Ivy May* now lies waiting to be preserved by the National Museum of Wales. [Alec Jones]

ANNO TRICESIMO PRIMO

Georgii III. Regis.

C A P. LXXXV.

An Act for making and maintaining a Canal or Navigable Communication from or near a certain Place called *Abernant*, in the County of *Glamorgan*, to and through a certain Place called *The Brickfield*, near *Melincrythan Pill*, into the River of *Neath*, near the Town of *Neath*, in the said County.

WHEREAS the making and maintaining a Canal or Navigable Communication for the Navigation of Boats, Barges, and other Vessels, from or near a certain Place called Abernant, in the County of Glamorgan, to and through a certain Place called The Brickfield, near Melincrythan Pill, into the River of Neath, near the Town of Neath, in the said County, will open Communications with several extensive Mines, Quarries, Woods, Iron Works, and Collieries, and be of great Utility: And whereas the several Persons herein-after named are desirous, at their own

Preamble.

Newly-launched *Ivy May* lying alongside the Neath Canal Co's old clay boat, Tynyrheol Lock, Tonna, 1934.
[Alec Jones]

Arthur Bowen, Bob Davies, and Will Evans, at work with the Neath Canal's weedcutter at Whitworth Arms, Clyne, in 1956.
[Author's Collection]

Aberdulais, looking south in 1959, showing the Neath Canal's junction with the Tennant. The Tennant Canal passes to Swansea under 'Pont Gam', the boatman's name for the curiously shaped junction bridge. The Vale of Neath Railway's bridge crosses the Neath Canal in the distance.

Inscribed stone on the towpath at Ynysbwllog, 1949. '... No person shall be permitted to ride or drive Cattle upon the towing path of the Canal except for the purpose of haling boats under the Penalty of Five Shillings for every Offence.'

Will Evans of Resolven, now aged 78, the retired foreman of the Neath Canal. He joined the staff in 1929 and served the company for 44 years. His store of canal lore is as impressive as his remarkable claim to have 'worn out five or six bikes' cycling the whole length of the towpath every day for 36 years.

Cast-iron aqueduct at Ynysbiban near Resolven with the inscription: NEATH ABBEY IRONWORKS GLAMORGANSHIRE 1835. The canal ran directly under the steep slopes of Craig Nedd and the aqueduct carried a fast stream safely over the navigation and into the adjoining river Neath.

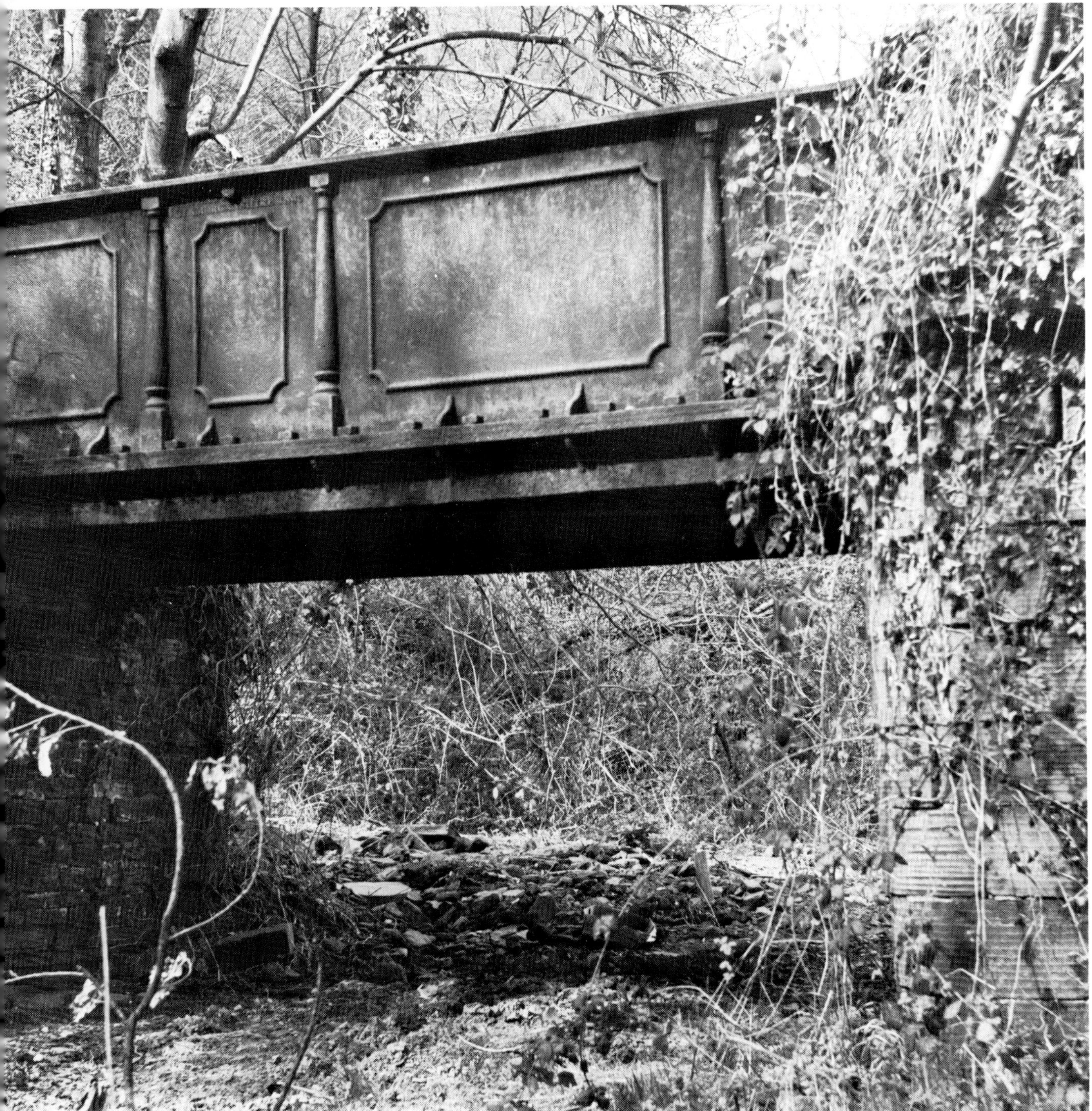

Ynysbwllog Aqueduct, near Clyne, in 1973, the principal engineering feature of the Neath Canal, showing four of the five stone arches spanning the river Neath.

42

A Neath Canal
Navigation
letterheading of 1949.
[Author's Collection]

At Maesmarchog, Glyn Neath, showing the top pound of the Neath Canal in 1937. The nearby canal head was the terminus of Tappenden's Tramroad to Hirwaun and Aberdare, which for a short time linked the Neath Canal with the Aberdare Canal. Tramroads also extended to Dinas Limestone Rocks and to gunpowder mills near Pont Nedd Fechan.

[Alec Jones]

Neath Canal Navigation

H. W. RICE-EVANS
Clerk and Manager

TELEPHONE NEATH 923

HWRE/IT.

Melyn Tinplate Works,
Neath

21st. May 1949.

Ian Lindsay Wright Esq.,
141, Whitchurch Road,
CARDIFF.

Canal cottage on the towpath of the Neath Canal at Resolven, 1974.

A motor coach negotiates the narrow hump-backed Lamb & Flag canal bridge at Glyn Neath just before it was widened in 1937. A successor to this route, the A465 Neath-Abergavenny Trunk road, threatens to obliterate parts of the Neath Canal.
[Alec Jones]

TENNANT CANAL

Edward Elton, owner of Glanywern Colliery in the 1780's, built a canal across Crymlyn Bog from his colliery eastwards to a shipping place at Trowman's Hole, now Red Jacket Pill, on the river Neath. Elton's canal, the Glanywern, was 3½ miles long, and was completed in 1790. In 1818 George Tennant leased the Glanywern Canal and extended and widened its lower end to form the Red Jacket Canal which connected the Neath river with the Tawe at what is now called Port Tennant (Swansea). Finally George Tennant completed his 'Neath & Swansea Junction Canal' in 1824 by extending the Red Jacket Canal northwards to Neath Abbey and Aberdulais, where a ten-arched aqueduct carried the canal over the river Neath to join the Neath Canal. The engineer was William Kirkhouse. The Tennant Canal main line was 8½ miles long with one lock at Aberdulais and the main cargoes carried were coal, timber, iron ore, and sand. Traffic increased to a maximum of 225,000 tons in 1866 and imports of copper ore from Chile kept the canal busy until the 1890's. Today the canal supplies water to industry, one of the main users being the B.P. oil refinery at Llandarcy, near Swansea. There has been no commercial traffic since the 1930's and most of the carrying had been lost to the Vale of Neath Railway by 1900.

A regular Neath-Swansea passenger packet boat service operated on the Tennant Canal between 1827 and 1850. This latter day excursion in a swept-out coal boat shows a Vale of Neath Sunday school party *en route* for the beach at Jersey Marine about 1910.
[Neath Antiquarian Society]

Neath became an important metallurgical centre in the sixteenth century and the Mines Royal Society began smelting copper ore at Neath Abbey in 1584. In 1798 the Neath Abbey Iron Co. was making pig-iron, using ironstone carried down the Neath Canal from Aberpergwm, and Neath Abbey was to develop into an important centre for iron making, engineering, and shipbuilding by the middle of the 19th century. This photograph, taken in 1949, shows the Tennant Canal where it passes in front of the monastic buildings of Neath Abbey. Nearby was the site of a short private branch canal to the ironworks.

Red Jacket Pill, a tidal creek of the river Neath opposite Giant's Grave, showing the barge lock at the end of the Red Jacket branch of the Tennant Canal, 1959.

George Gorvett of the Tennant Canal, who worked a daily schoolchildren's boat from the isolated Pritchard's Cottages to Jersey Marine between 1922 and 1937.

The remains of the boat *Sylvia*, of Neath or Tennant Canal origin, lying in the Tennant Canal south of Neath Bridge in 1949. The river Neath lies below the towpath on the right of the photograph.

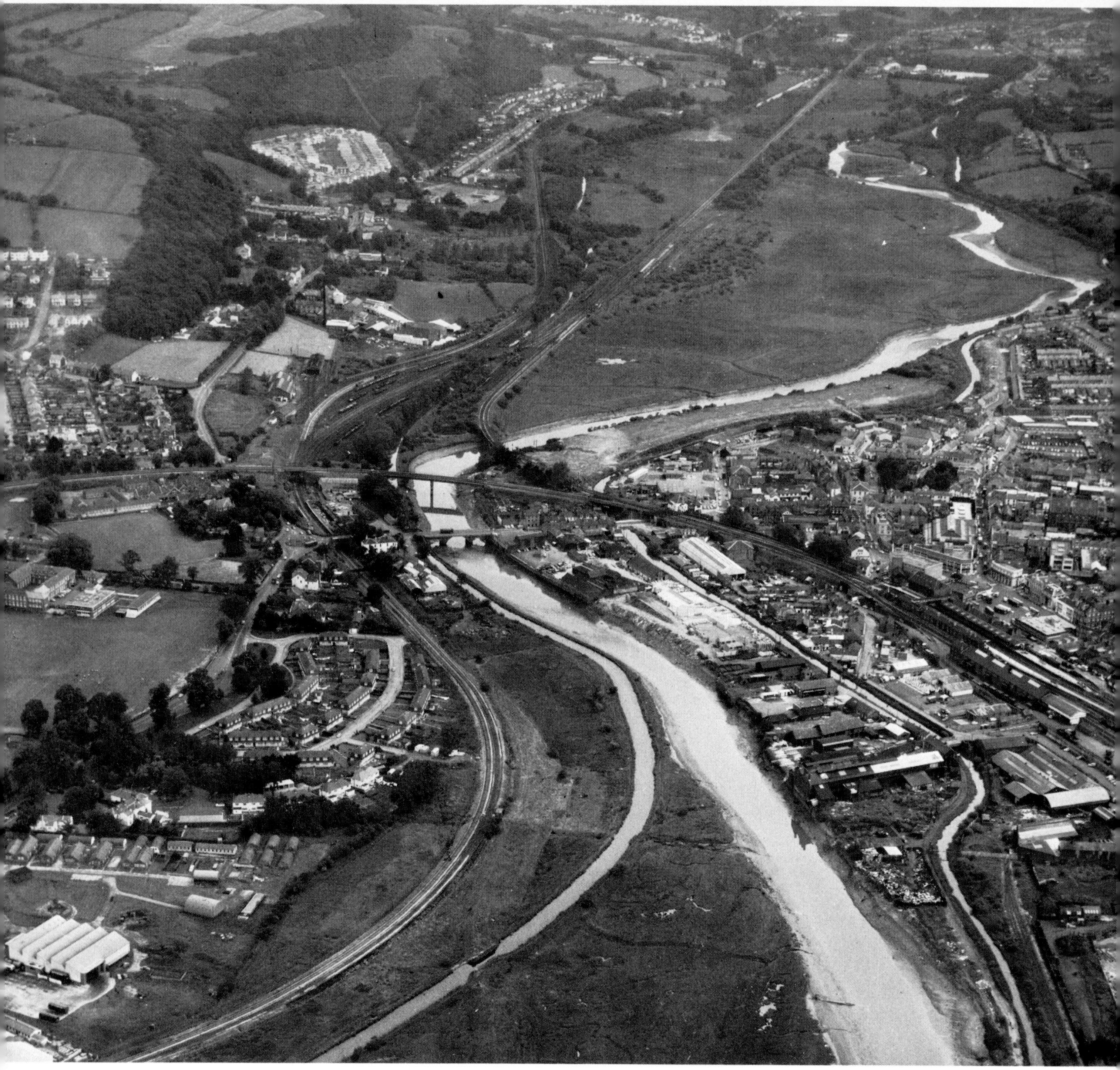

George Tennant's 340′ long aqueduct over the river Neath at Aberdulais, completed by William Kirkhouse in June 1824. Ten masonry arches span the river and there is a lock and a toll building at the far end where the canal descends towards Swansea. The Tennant Canal's principal feeder draws water from the weir on the right. The photograph was taken in 1949.

The three inland waterways of Neath, seen from the air in 1964. The tidal river Neath was navigable to small vessels as far as the quays at Neath Bridge, seen near the centre of the photograph. On the right, the Neath Canal follows the Vale of Neath to Aberdulais which is at the top of the picture. Curving in on the lower left is the Tennant Canal, which is closely paralleled by the Vale of Neath line of the Western Region. [Aerofilms Ltd.]

Street nameplate at Canal Side, Aberdulais, a canal bank community.

Dredging the Tennant Canal at Canal Side, Aberdulais, in 1973. The dumper is standing near the canal's maintenance depot, which is built over the entrance to the Dulais branch canal.

'None but botanists traverse this morass . . .' (Nicholson's *Cambrian Traveller's Guide,* 1840). The author's boat among reeds and water irises, a few hundred yards up the Glanywern Canal in the windswept and desolate Crymlyn Bog in 1949.

A passenger train standing in Pont Yates station, in 1951, on the site of the Kidwelly & Llanelly Canal. The second coach is a G.W.R. low roof vehicle specially built to pass under the Burry Port line's canal bridges.

KIDWELLY & LLANELLY CANAL

Thomas Kymer obtained the first Welsh canal Act in 1766 for a Canal from Kidwelly Quay to his coal mines at Carway in the Gwendraeth Fawr valley. Kymer's Canal was three miles long and was opened in 1769. By about 1824 the Kidwelly & Llanelly Canal and Tramroad Co. had added branches across Pembrey Marshes and by 1838, a nine mile long canal existed from Pontyberem to Burry Port, using water-powered inclined planes designed by James Green. The K & L Co. turned itself into a railway company in 1865 and converted its canal into a railway, forming the Burry Port & Gwendraeth Valley line of the G.W.R. Llanelli (to give the town its modern spelling), was never reached by the canal.

A (mis-spelt) B.P.G.V.R. cast iron notice at Cwmmawr station, 1950. From Pontyberem to Cwmmawr the canal was probably never completed and a coal tramroad was laid along the towpath.

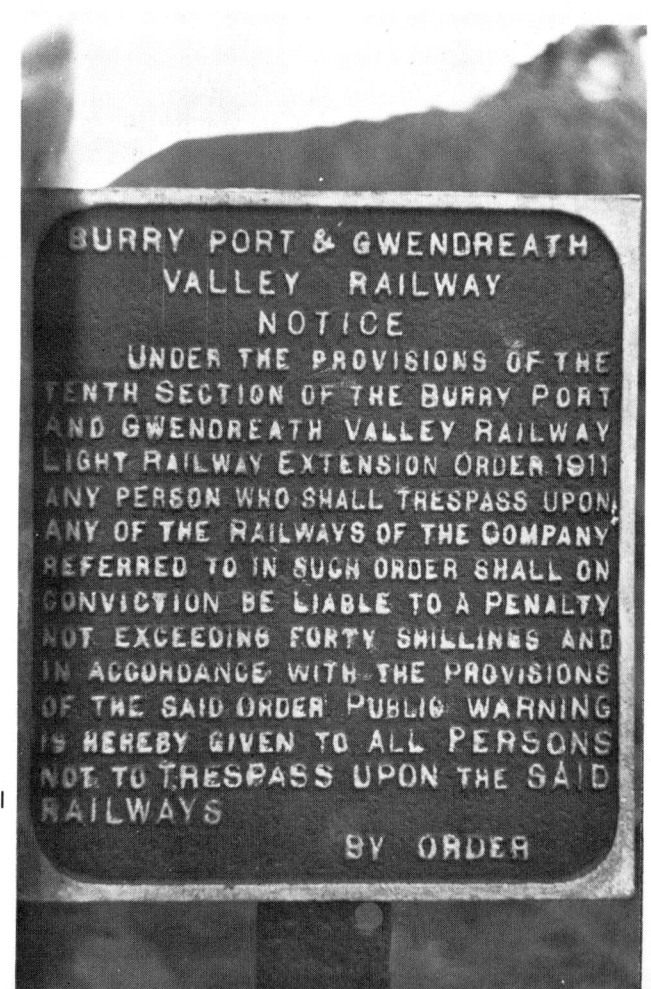

52

Kidwelly & Llanelly Canal bridges were adapted for railway use after 1865. This one at the site of Craiglon Bridge halt, near Pembrey, is characteristically flooded.

The original Kidwelly & Llanelly Canal aqueduct of 1815 near Trimsaran, photographed in 1973. This masonry structure, which crosses the Gwendraeth Fawr river, is still carrying the anthracite coal traffic of the Western Region's Burry Port & Gwendraeth Valley line.

SWANSEA CANAL

The Swansea Canal Act of 1794 authorised a canal from the Brewery Bank in Swansea up the Tawe Valley for sixteen miles to Hen Neuadd near Abercrave, Breconshire (now part of Powys). The canal passed through Clydach, Pontardawe, Ystalyfera, and Ystradgynlais, and there were 36 locks taking boats 67' long, 7' 6" wide, and carrying up to 25 tons. A short section at Landore—the Trewyddfa Canal—was built and owned by the Duke of Beaufort. Thomas Sheasby engineered the greater part of the canal, which was completed to Hen Neuadd in 1798.

Coal and iron were the main cargoes carried to Swansea for export from the transhipment wharves serving vessels lying in the river Tawe. The Swansea Vale (later Midland) Railway reached Ystalyfera in 1859 and drew off much of the canal's traffic and in 1872 the Great Western Railway bought the canal and encouraged a profitable traffic on it for more than twenty years. It ceased to carry trade in 1931 but was a useful source of industrial water supply until recent years. The British Transport Commission abandoned sections of the Swansea Canal in 1949 and 1957, and the remaining Pontardawe-Morriston section of it is administered by the British Waterways Board.

Vivian & Sons' boat No. 12, still bearing its owner's engraved plate, *V & S Ltd. Colliery No. 12,* when lying derelict at Cefn on the G.W.R. Monmouthshire Canal Crumlin Arm in 1950. The G.W.R. bought a number of Swansea boats in the late 1920's and transferred them by rail to the Monmouthshire & Brecon and the Kennet & Avon Canals for maintenance use. At 65' 0" long by 7' 6" beam, the Swansea boats were the nearest South Wales equivalent to the straight-sided 'day boat' narrow boats of the Birmingham Canal Navigations. [Derek Chaplin]

Industrial Swansea. This record of a boat and horse alongside the Hafod chemical works in 1921 is one of the few 'live' Swansea Canal photographs in existence. The Swansea end of the canal was highly industrialised and served numerous copper and spelter works, collieries, patent fuel and chemical works, and the Cornish family of Vivian, originally of Truro, established the famous Hafod copper smelting works here in 1810. Vivian & Sons owned a fleet of canal boats for bringing coal from their collieries to the works, though this boat, reputedly the last to work on the canal, was probably owned by S. & J. Hill of Clydach. [National Museum of Wales]

CANALS of SOUTH WALES

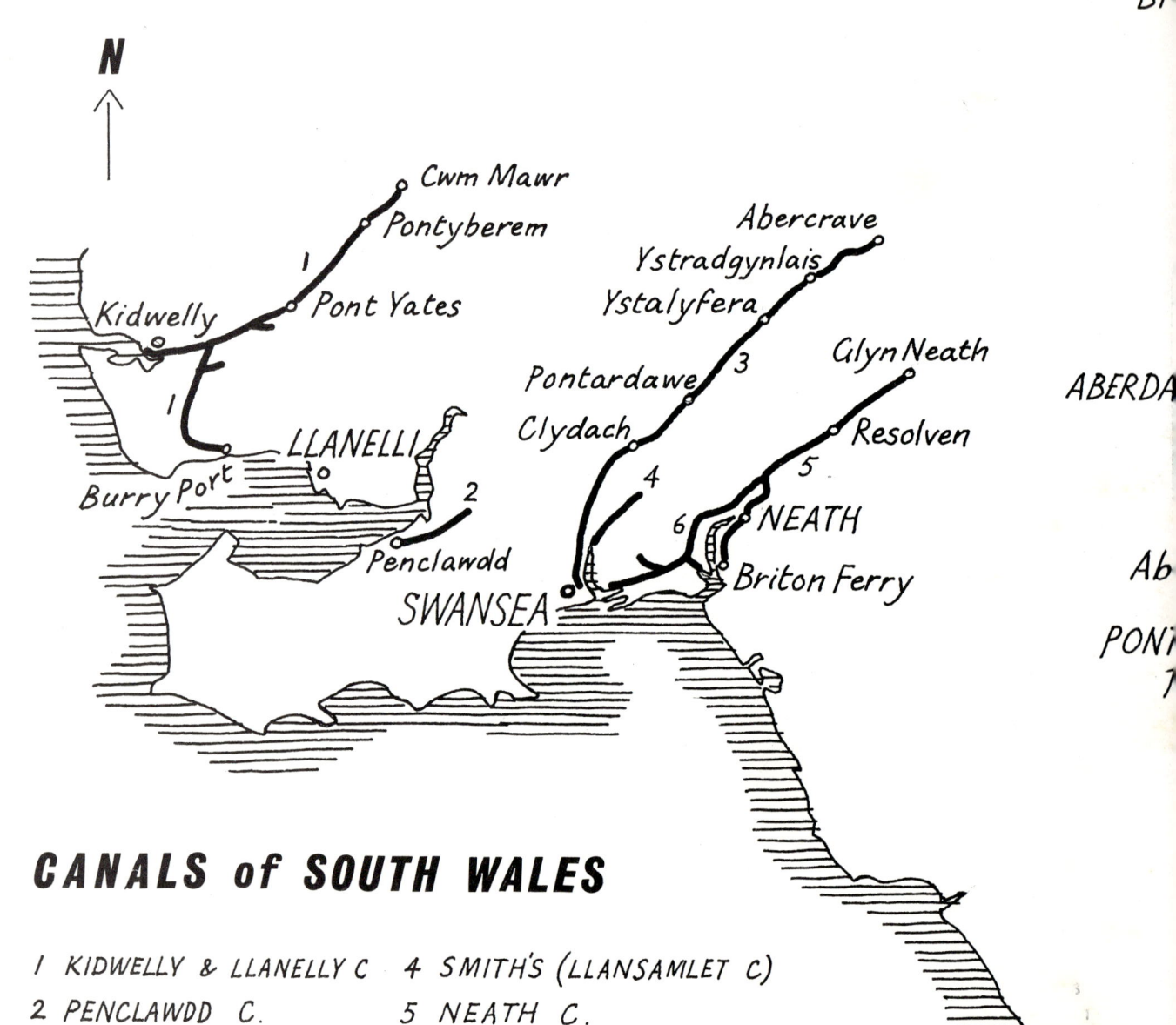

1. KIDWELLY & LLANELLY C
2. PENCLAWDD C.
3. SWANSEA C.
4. SMITH'S (LLANSAMLET C)
5. NEATH C.
6. TENNANT C.

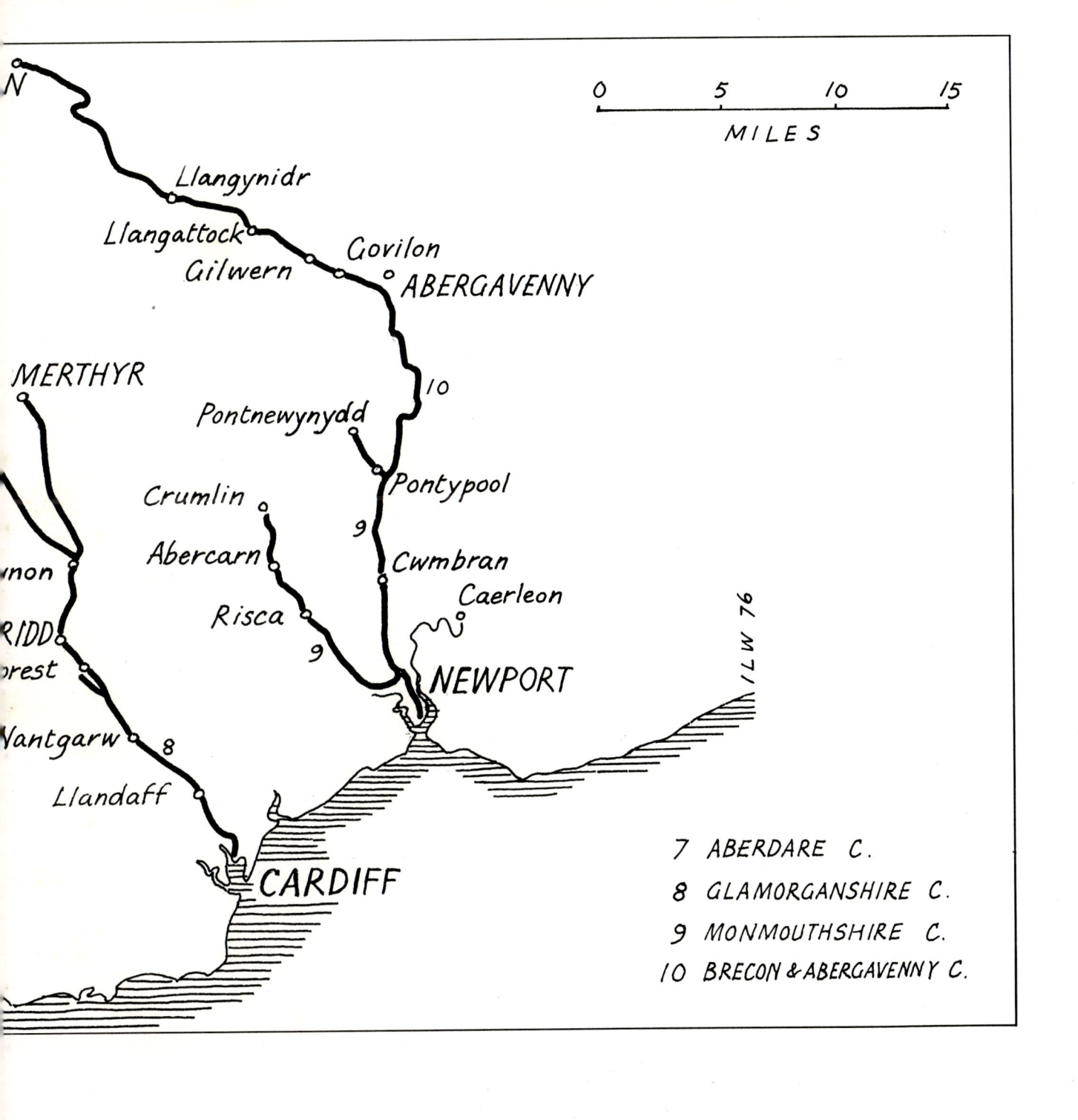

7 ABERDARE C.
8 GLAMORGANSHIRE C.
9 MONMOUTHSHIRE C.
10 BRECON & ABERGAVENNY C.

A solitary ketch, thought to be the *Democrat* of Barnstaple, at Weaver's warehouse in the North Dock basin at Swansea in the summer of 1949. Her trade between Swansea and North Devon was in flour and animal feedstuffs, though she also carried basic slag. The North Dock was a floating harbour completed in 1851 by converting the town reach of the river Tawe and completing a New Cut for river traffic serving the copper wharves at Hafod and Landore. The Swansea Canal was connected to the North Dock by a canal branch which went out of use when the dock was closed and filled in during the 1930's, but the North Dock basin survived for a few years after the Second World War.

An Andrew Barclay saddle tank of John Player's Tinplate works, Clydach, pauses on the canal bridge at Cwm Clydach lock in this view from the author's boat in 1949. Clydach was the end of the Swansea Canal's four mile lockless stretch from Landore. Although horse traction was the usual mode on the Swansea, the four mile level encouraged one trader to use steam tugs for hauling boats between locks. The canal became disused in the thirties but in 1936 it was reported that fourteen tinplate works in the Tawe Valley were entirely dependent on the canal for water.

Pontardawe in 1973, with one of the few lengths of the Swansea Canal remaining in existence. Reflected in its waters is St. Peter's church, the gift of tinplate manufacturer and canal freighter William Parsons in 1860. At nearby Cae'r Doc, boats were built and launched.

The picturesque towpath bridge over the entrance to the private Yniscedwyn Ironworks branch canal near Gurnos in 1949, looking down the Swansea Canal towpath to Ystalyfera. This was also the terminus of the Brecon Forest Tramroad from Sennybridge.

The 177'-long Gurnos Aqueduct over the river Twrch at Ystalyfera, the largest engineering structure on the Swansea Canal. Built about 1797, it was still intact when this photograph was taken in 1974.

Lamb & Flag Bridge at Hen Neuadd, near Abercrave, at the head of the Swansea Canal, 1949. The canal, 372 above sea level, terminated beyond the bridge at a basin and ironworks. The site, disused since well before 1900, also marked the end of two tramroads from Cribarth limestone quarries.

The Canal Co's water-wheel at Thick's Locks, Godre'r graig, near Ystalyfera, in 1959. The wheel powered the machinery of the carpenter's shop, water being admitted from the canal through the paddle in the foreground. The G.W.R. prolonged the life of the wheel with a bracing of chains which were pulled tight with Swindon screw couplings.

MONMOUTHSHIRE & BRECON CANAL

In 1880 the Great Western Railway took control of the Monmouthshire Railway & Canal Co's 42 miles of canal from Newport to Brecon and the 11 mile branch canal from Malpas (Newport) to Crumlin. This G.W.R. system had originated as two separate undertakings—the Monmouthshire Canal, built under an Act of 1792, and the Brecknock & Abergavenny Canal, authorised in 1793. The Monmouthshire Canal was a prosperous concern with a monopoly of the coal and iron traffic passing to Newport for export. The company duplicated parts of its canal routes with parallel tramroads, operated locomotives on them and later converted them to modern railways. In 1849 the company changed its name to the Monmouthshire Railway and Canal Co. and, to secure the remaining traffic to its Newport & Pontypool Railway, it bought the Brecknock & Abergavenny Canal in 1865. After this time the canal went into decline. The Monmouthshire Canal's main line ran from the river Usk in Newport to Pontnewynydd, north of Pontypool, rising by 42 locks in 11 miles, and was opened in 1796. The Crumlin Arm, opened in 1799, climbed through 32 locks in 11 miles, and the engineer for the Monmouthshire was Thomas Dadford, Junior.

The Brecon & Abergavenny Canal was opened for traffic between Gilwern and Brecon in 1800 with Thomas Dadford as engineer, but was not completed southwards to join the Monmouthshire Canal at Pontymoile (Pontypool) until 1812. Tramroads connected the canal with ironworks at the heads of the mining valleys such as Nantyglo and Blaenavon, and iron, limestone, and coal were the principal cargoes carried, some of this passing inland by tramroad to Hereford and to Hay and Eardisley.

Under G.W.R. control the Monmouthshire & Brecon Canal had ceased to be used commercially by 1939 but it survived the war as a supplier of water to industry. The canal passed to the British Transport Commission in 1948 and in 1949 the Crumlin Arm was closed, to be followed by the rest of the Monmouthshire main line by Acts of 1954 and 1962. The old Brecon & Abergavenny section, now isolated among mountains, has been fully restored to navigation with the financial assistance of the two local authorities. Scenically one of the most beautiful canals in Britain, it lies within the Brecon Beacons National Park, and has been part of the British Waterways Board's undertaking since 1963.

G.W.R. Monmonthshire & Brecon Canal licence plate issued to pleasure-boat owners. Issued in 1947, it authorised use over the whole system but powered craft and the use of locks were prohibited.
[Author's Collection]

Moderator Wharf, near the bottom of Corn Street in Newport, on the Monmouthshire Canal, in 1915. The photograph shows Jones & Co's last market boat loading goods for Abercarn and Crumlin. The proprietor, George Jobbins, ran two boats weekly on the Crumlin Arm and one boat to Brecon. In January 1915 this 120 year old business was closed down and the boatmen enlisted for war service in France.

[Newport Public Library]

A summer idyll of about 1900; Allt-yr-ynn on the Crumlin Arm near Newport, beloved of the poet W. H. Davies. The bridge is M.R. & C. Co. No. 140 (later G.W.R. No. 3) on the ascent from Malpas to Cefn. The lock gate in the foreground clearly demonstrates the Monmouthshire Canal arrangement for filling a lock—a single top gate paddle with vertical rack, and two ground paddles operated from wooden jack posts.
[Author's Collection]

In Memoriam card to a canal reservoir tragedy of 1875. 'Through the bursting of Cwm Carne Reservoir near Cross Keys . . . on July 14 1875, the residence of Mr. J. Hunt, flannel manufacturer, was swept away, and the whole of his family, with two servants and an apprentice boy, were drowned.' Cwmcarn Reservoir was one of three supplying water to the upper pounds of the Crumlin Arm.
[Author's Collection]

CWM CARNE, 1875.

"The Rain descended and the Floods came . . . . and beat upon that House, and it fell, and great was the fall of it."—Matt. vii. 27.

In Remembrance

Of those who perished by the Flood of July 14th, 1875.

	AGED		AGED
JOHN HUNT	47 Years.	ELIZABETH WEEKS	17 Years.
MARY ANN HUNT	52 ,,	MARY JONES	15 ,,
JOHN HUNT	23 ,,	GEORGE KLIEN	15 ,,
LETITIA HUNT	21 ,,	HOWELL DAVIES	60 ,,
ELIZABETH HUNT	19 ,,	MARGARET DAVIES	38 ,,
JAMES HUNT	11 ,,	JOHN DAVIES	30 ,,

Through the bursting of the Cwm Carne Reservoir, near Cross Keys, Monmouthshire (on the night of Wednesday, July 14th, 1875) the residence of Mr. J. Hunt, Flannel Manufacturer, was swept away, and the whole of his family, with two servants and an apprentice boy, were drowned. Mr. Hunt was saved in a tree, but died on Sunday, July 18th, from injuries received in the catastrophe. John Foley, an apprentice boy, is the only survivor.

A Cottage was also destroyed, and the inmates, HOWELL DAVIES, his Daughter, and Son, were all drowned

The Monmouthshire Canal at Darran Bridge, Risca, in 1948, on the five mile pound of the Crumlin Arm between Rogerstone and Cwmcarn. Although officially abandoned in 1949, several miles of the arm still exist. The line is steeply terraced along the mountainside above the river Ebbw, and its rise over the eleven miles from Malpas to Crumlin was 353'.

A street nameplate at Risca near the site of Navigation Bridge.

A steep ascent over the arch of G.W.R. Bridge No. 4 on the Crumlin Arm at Newport, 1973.

A Monmouthshire Canal boat passes under Crindau Bridge, the first out of Newport, on its way towards Malpas Junction. The photograph was taken about 1914.

Near Mill Street sidings, Newport, about 1914, showing a boat loaded with coal for the brickworks at Allt-yr-ynn on the Monmouthshire Canal's Crumlin Arm. The parallel railway is the former M.R. & C. Co's line from Pontypool to Newport and the wooden structure over the canal is a remarkable double drawbridge carrying the rails of the access siding to Cordes Dos Nail Works. [British Transport Commission]

Cast-iron plate of the M.R. & C. Co at the Waterways Museum, Stoke Bruerne, Northamptonshire.

Newport's canal tunnel; a view inside the short Barrack Hill Tunnel in 1974.

Iron post on the towpath at Risca, in use as a bollard. The design of this post, which is scored by the rubbing of boat tow-ropes, suggests that it is a reject cannon from a Monmouthshire ironworks.

Five Locks, Cwmbran, on the Monmouthshire Canal main line in the summer of 1949. Lock 63, at the top of this flight, marks the present limit of the derelict section through Pontypool and Sebastopol.

Milepost at Pontymoile indicating 9 miles from Potter Street lock, Newport. The canal was cut back to a terminus at Llanarth Street, Newport, in 1879 and the company's mileposts were re-positioned.   [Gordon Rattenbury]

Bridge, toll house, and site of the stop lock at Pontymoile Junction, where the Brecon & Abergavenny Canal joins the Monmouthshire. Out of sight to the left, the Monmouthshire Canal ends in a basin, but originally ascended through Pontypool to a terminus at Pontnewynydd. The attractive round forms of the B & A toll house echo the prevailing Regency style of 1812.

BRECON & ABERGAVENNY CANAL

The last of the South Wales canals to survive as a navigable waterway. Now detached from Newport by the abandonment of the Monmouthshire Canal, this beautiful and remote canal has been fully restored for navigation between Jockey Bridge, Pontypool, and Brecon, and was officially reopened by the Minister of State for Wales in 1970. The restoration programme, which gained a Prince of Wales Award, was carried out by the British Waterways Board with the financial help of the Monmouthshire and Brecon County Councils, who were motivated no doubt by the canal's unique position in a designated National Park. The canal is 33 miles long and gains almost all its elevation from the Monmouthshire Canal, running for 25 miles at the 367' level and rising to a summit of 427' in Brecon. There are five locks at Llangynidr and one at Brynich, as well as several aqueducts. Water supply is drawn from the river Usk at Brecon and is important to industry in the Pontypool area. However, in March 1975 a disastrous burst occurred at Llanfoist which closed parts of the canal and through traffic is still suspended.

Edwardian summer; a Sunday school outing by boat—with crates of minerals on the foredeck—passing the wharf at Llangattock about 1908. Local boat outings were traditional on all South Wales canals and on the Monmouthshire & Brecon they continued as late as 1946, using boats hired from the G.W.R. This craft, which belonged to a private trader, shows rare evidence of South Wales boat decoration. The bow and stern plates are painted with lozenges and crescents. [Welsh Folk Museum, St. Fagans]

Sign at the Navigation Inn, Gilwern, one-time boatman's pub on the Brecon & Abergavenny Canal, where the Abergavenny to Brynmawr road crosses the canal.

Llanfoist Wharf near Abergavenny in 1974, showing the iron warehouse once used by the Blaenavon Co. Nearby are the remains of Hill's Tramroad inclines descending Blorenge Mountain from Blaenavon.

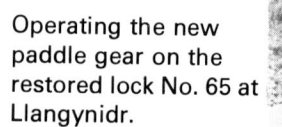

Operating the new paddle gear on the restored lock No. 65 at Llangynidr.

Govilon Wharf and moorings of the Govilon Boat Club, the only inland cruising club on Welsh canals. At Govilon, where the British Waterways Board has a section office, the canal was crossed by the L.M.S. Abergavenny-Merthyr line, which had an exchange siding whence coal was boated to Llangattock by Morgan of Llangynidr until about 1933.

Lock 65 and the British Waterways Board's Cwm Crawnon maintenance yard at Llangynidr, in 1974.

The wharf cottage—now demolished—at Clydach basin, Gilwern, terminus of the Beaufort and Llammarch tramroads.

Late Victorian Sunday school excursion on the Brecon & Abergavenny Canal at Gilwern. South Wales canal boats were normally wood-built and this iron-hulled craft is a comparative rarity.

Canal and rail at Talybont-on-Usk. A Sunday morning engineers' train on the Brecon & Merthyr line of the Western Region crosses the canal at White Hart Bridge on the seven mile climb to Torpantau, 1 September 1963. The lonely Brecon & Abergavenny Canal was crossed by railways only twice in its 33 miles. Ironically it has survived both competitors.
[B. J. Ashworth]

Thomas Dadford's four-arched stone aqueduct over the Usk at Brynich, opened for traffic in 1800. Locks were out of action and motor craft were banned when this photograph was taken in 1952. The G.W.R. boat at the far end of the aqueduct is ex-Swansea Canal (Vivian & Sons No. 48), and was reputedly the last boat through the locks at Llangynidr.

G.W.R. Monmouthshire & Brecon milepost at Brecon, indicating 42 miles from Llanarth Street, Newport.

Canal bank cottages on the wide towpath between Watton Wharf and the head of the canal at Brecon.
[Peter Norton]

Tramroad and canal bridges at Watton Wharf, Brecon, in 1949. On the right is Watton Bridge of the Brecon & Abergavenny Canal. The arch on the left was used by the Hay Railway, an important tramroad opened to Hay in 1816 for the distribution of canalborne coal, lime, and limestone.

79

A Llanfoist-based hire cruiser approaches the 'bridge hole' of Panteg Bridge near Llangynidr in 1968, the year agreement was reached for the canal's restoration within the Brecon Beacons National Park. In G.W.R. days there were 114 canal bridges on the Brecon & Abergavenny Canal, the number plates from No. 101 upwards having the characteristic Swindon cast-iron numerals. [Alan Fowler]

On Chirk Aqueduct in the 1920's, the narrow boat *Starling* crosses from England into Wales with the river Ceiriog flowing 70' below. Opened in 1801, the aqueduct is a stone-arched structure carrying the Llangollen Canal in a cast-iron trough. Ahead lies the 459 yard Chirk Tunnel. On the left is the Chirk viaduct of the G.W.R. Shrewsbury-Chester line.
[Harry Arnold Collection]

LLANGOLLEN CANAL

The Welsh section of the Shropshire Union Canal begins at Hurleston on the S.U. Wolverhampton-Chester main line near Nantwich and heads towards Wales through Whitchurch and Ellesmere. At Welsh Frankton (29 miles), the derelict Montgomery Canal branches off towards Newtown. The Llangollen Canal runs its spectacular course into Wales at Chirk, and crosses the famous Chirk and Pontcysyllte aqueducts to reach the beautiful Vale of Llangollen. Begun under the Ellesmere Canal Act of 1793 with Jessop and Telford as engineers, the project was intended to link Shrewsbury and Chester by way of the ironworks and collieries of Ruabon and Wrexham. Only parts of the scheme were realised and the Ellesmere Canal spent an isolated existence distributing coal, limestone, iron, and agricultural traffic within Shropshire and Montgomeryshire. In 1805 the Ellesmere finally reached Chester by an extension to the old Chester Canal at Hurleston. It was also linked across the Dee to Trevor where tramroads connected it to Ruabon. The Llangollen Canal's role as a water feeder from the Dee accounts for its survival. Now part of the British Waterways Board's network, it is a popular route for holiday cruisers in the season.

Captain Jones of Llangollen, operating one of his horse-drawn trip boats near the Horseshoe Falls at Llantisilio about 1900. The tourist potential of the Llangollen Canal was realised as early as 1884, when the first passenger boat trip business was founded.
[Borough of Wirral: Wallasey Library]

Wonder of the Waterways; Pontcysyllte Aqueduct, Telford's masterpiece, strides across the Dee near Trevor in Clwyd, carrying the Llangollen Canal in an iron trough 120' up in the sky. 'The most impressive work of art I have ever seen' was Sir Walter Scott's estimate of it. Completed in 1805, Pontcysyllte took ten years to build.

Black Park Colliery Basin at Chirk in 1952, seen through the arch of the towpath bridge. This canal dock, built in 1805, was reached by the extreme end of the 2' 4½" gauge Glyn Valley Tramway.
[Derek Chaplin]

Crossing Pontcysyllte; a T.V. cameraman records Shropshire Union boatman Jack Roberts bow-hauling a Railway & Canal Historical Society party across the aqueduct during a narrow boat excursion led by the late E. A. Wilson of Ellesmere in 1956.
[J. A. Hall]

Antwerp, a British Waterways horse-drawn narrow boat used on maintenance duties along the Welsh Section of the Shropshire Union in the 1950's.
[J. A. Hall]

Ellesmere Maintenance Yard in 1952. Within the yard are the original Ellesmere Company's office (Beech House) plus the workshops and dry dock. The boat is a Shropshire Union ice-breaker.
[Derek Chaplin]

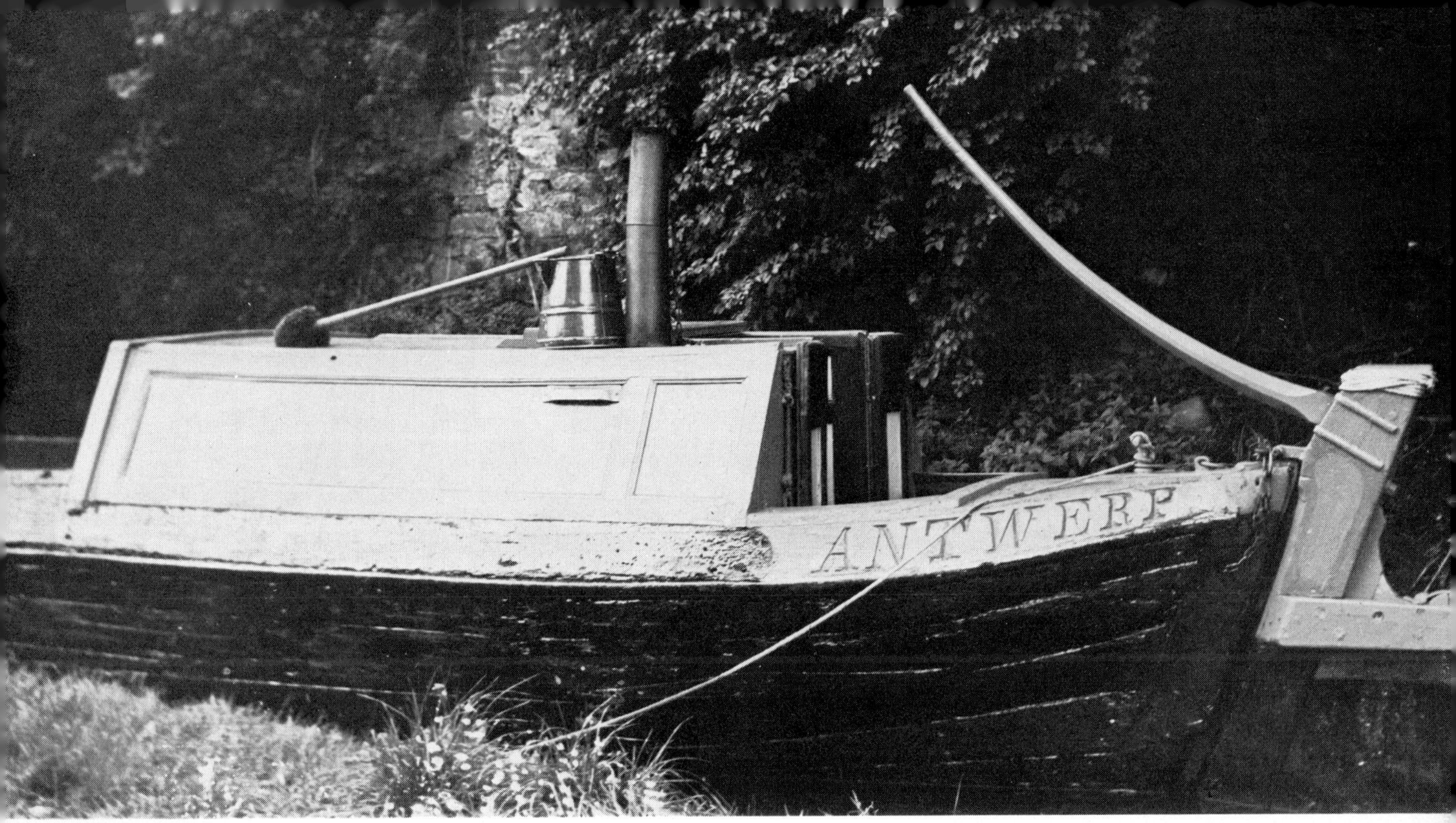
ANTWERP

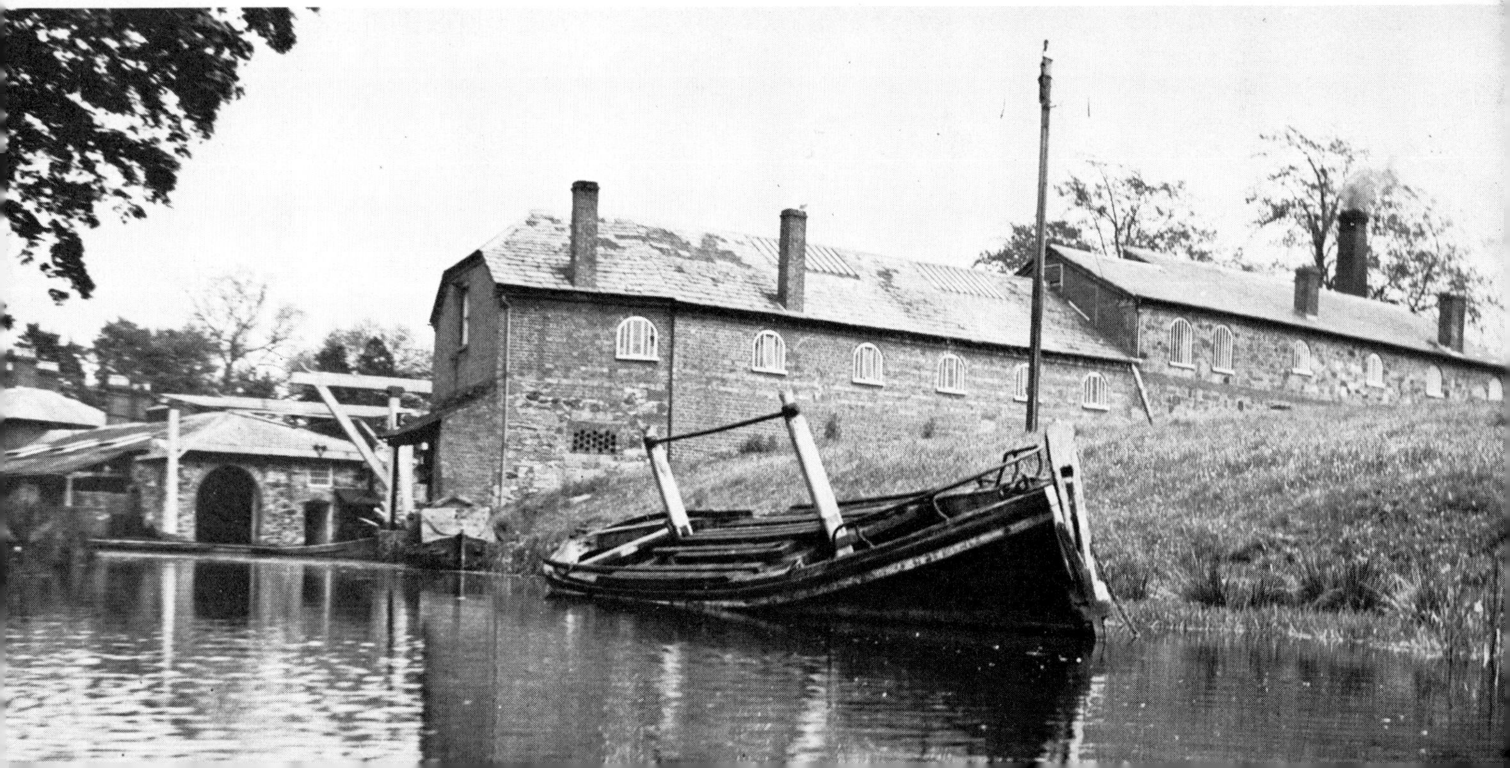

David Wain's Canal Exhibition in the former S.U. warehouse at Llangollen wharf, run in connection with Welsh Canal Holiday Craft's Llangollen horse-drawn pleasure boat trips. This mural, which was painted by Tony Lewery, depicts a wharf scene and two traditional types of inland waterway craft. [Welsh Canal Holiday Craft]

The hotel boats *Jupiter* and *Saturn* of Preston Brook about to cross Chirk Aqueduct on a Llangollen Canal holiday cruise. Both these craft are conversions from working narrow boats. *Saturn,* like L.T.C. Rolt's famous *Cressy,* was a wood-built boat from the Shropshire Union.

[Harry Arnold]

Ellesmere Basin at the end of the short Ellesmere Arm, 1952. The message on the warehouse was a mere 31 years out of date, the S.U.R. & C. Co. having ceased carrying in 1921 and disposed of its boats to other traders. [Derek Chaplin]

The Shropshire Union Railways & Canal Co. (leased in 1847 to the L.N.W.R.) had been formed from a merger of the Ellesmere & Chester, Montgomery, Shrewsbury, and Birmingham & Liverpool Junction Canals. The S.U. began carrying on its Autherley-Ellesmere Port main line and on its Middlewich branch, and in 1849 this was extended to the whole 200 mile system which included the Ellesmere and Montgomery Canals. The L.N.W.R. encouraged the boat services since much of the system lay in rival railway territory. The services were augmented by 'fly boats' running to regular schedules.

On its Welsh Canals the S.U. was handling limestone traffic from Trevor and Llanymynech to the ironworks of Wellington and Oakengates, and returning to Ruabon with iron ore from Golden Hill near Burslem. There was also a coal trade from Ruabon collieries to Chester and Ellesmere Port and a traffic in granite and slate. Fly boats were operated to Llangollen and Newtown. In 1889 the S.U. owned 395 narrow boats and its main lines were worked vigorously until the end of the first World War. The Welsh Section traffic had long been in decline, and was much reduced by the opening of the Oswestry & Newtown Railway.

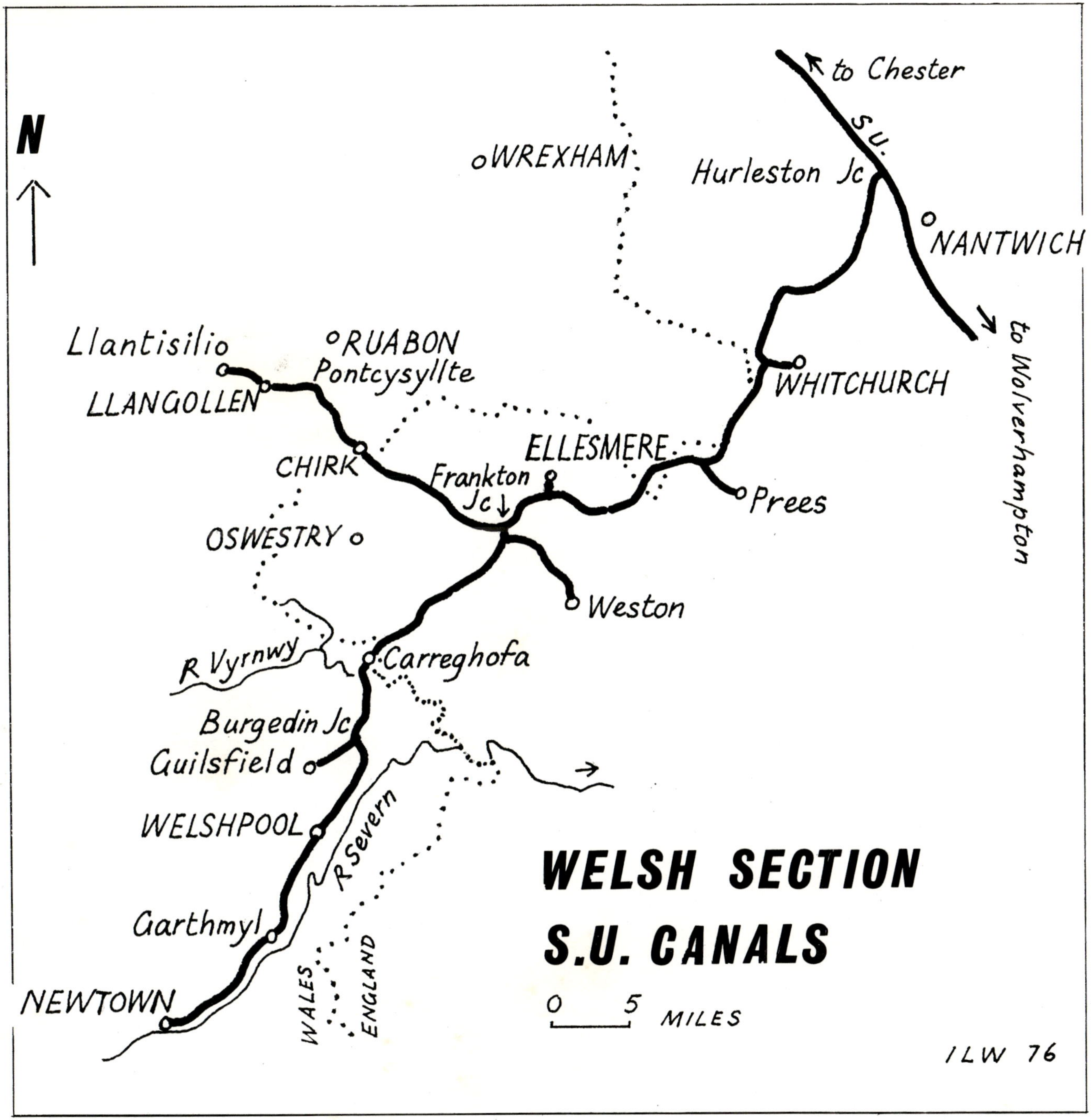
N
to Chester
S.U.
oWREXHAM
Hurleston Jc
NANTWICH
to Wolverhampton
Llantisilio
RUABON
Pontcysyllte
LLANGOLLEN
WHITCHURCH
ELLESMERE
CHIRK
Frankton Jc
Prees
OSWESTRY
Weston
R Vyrnwy
Carreghofa
Burgedin Jc
Guilsfield
WELSHPOOL
R Severn
Garthmyl
NEWTOWN
WALES
ENGLAND
WELSH SECTION
S.U. CANALS
0 5 MILES
ILW 76

MONTGOMERYSHIRE CANAL

The 35 miles of derelict waterway running from Frankton to Llanymynech, Pool Quay, Welshpool, and on to Newtown are commonly called the Montgomeryshire Canal, but in fact the whole Newtown Arm of the Shropshire Union was built and run originally by three different companies. The first section, from Frankton to Carreghofa, was the 11 miles of the Ellesmere Canal, completed in 1796. Then follows the 16 miles of the Montgomeryshire Canal Eastern Branch, from Carreghofa to Garthmyl, with the two mile Guilsfield branch. The final section, which did not join the S.U. until 1850, was the Montgomeryshire Canal Western Branch, opened to Newtown in 1821. The Montgomery was a mainly agricultural canal with a major concern in carrying coal and limestone, though in 1836 a fly-boat service was working between Newtown and London. In 1936, while under L.M.S. Railway control, a burst in the banks occurred near Frankton. The damage was never repaired and in 1944 the L.M.S. officially abandoned the canal which has lain derelict ever since. In 1967 the Shropshire Union Canal Society investigated the possibility of reopening the Montgomery for navigation. A length in Welshpool was cleared and restored by the Society and Welshpool Lock was officially reopened by the Prince of Wales in May 1974.

Waiting to be restored; Carreghofa Lock No. 2 on the derelict Montgomeryshire Canal beyond Llanymynech.

William Jeffreys; Shropshire Union Canal pensioner living at the wharf by the Vyrnwy Aqueduct. He worked at Maesbury Marsh warehouse in 1921.

Jungle conditions; a tree and nest take over the wharf crane at Tyddyn Basin, at the end of the Guilsfield branch.

The unusual cast-iron ground paddle gear at the head of Carreghofa Lock.

Derelict locks of the Montgomeryshire Canal, looking towards the junction with the Llangollen Canal at Welsh Frankton, 1956.
[J. A. Hall]

The narrow boat *Berriew,* trapped on the wrong side of the 1936 burst, quietly rots away among the reeds at Belan Locks.
[Harry Arnold]

Symbol of hope; *Powis Princess,* the passenger narrow boat operated by the Shropshire Union Canal Society, brings new life to the restored stretch of the Montgomery Canal through Welshpool.
[Harry Arnold]

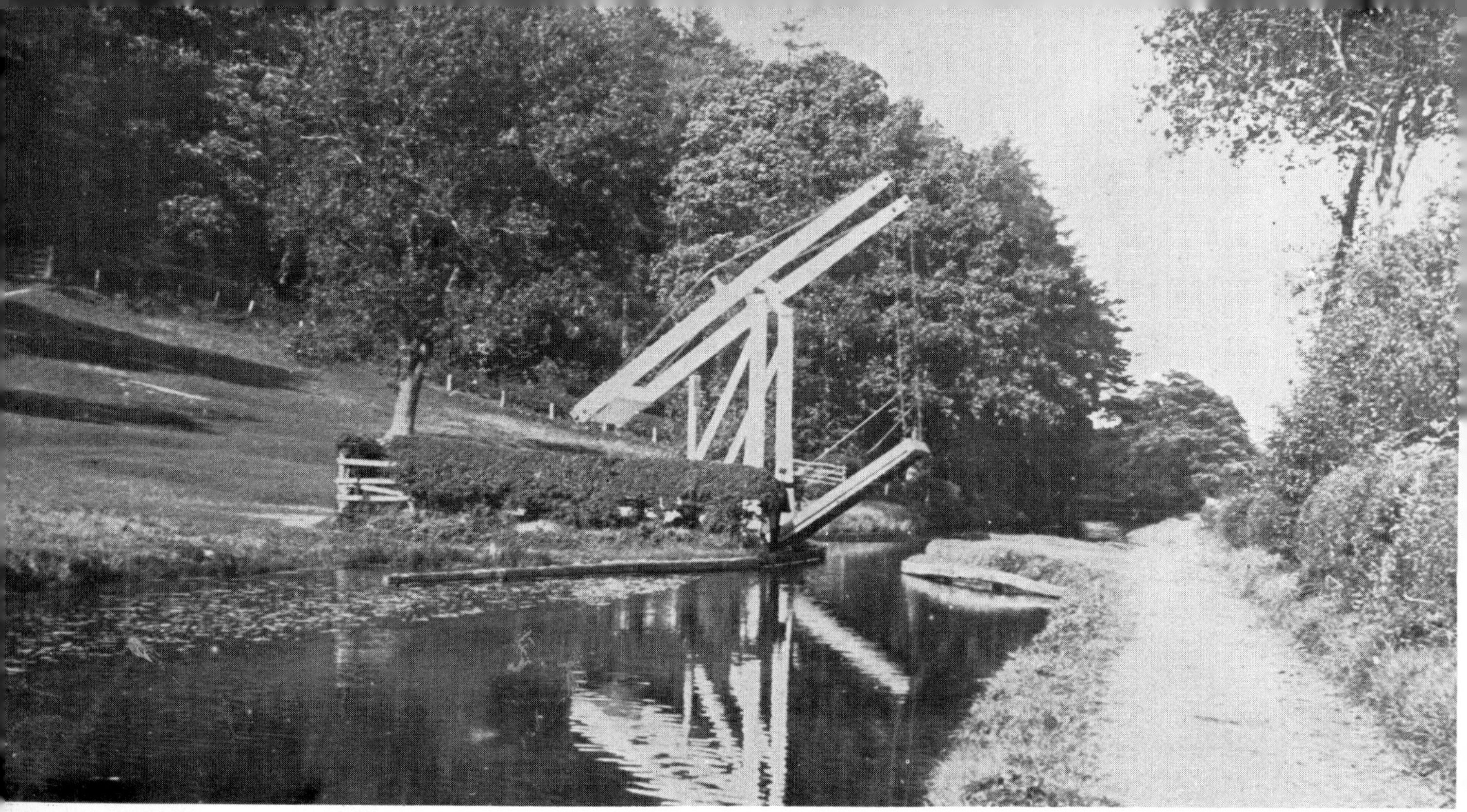

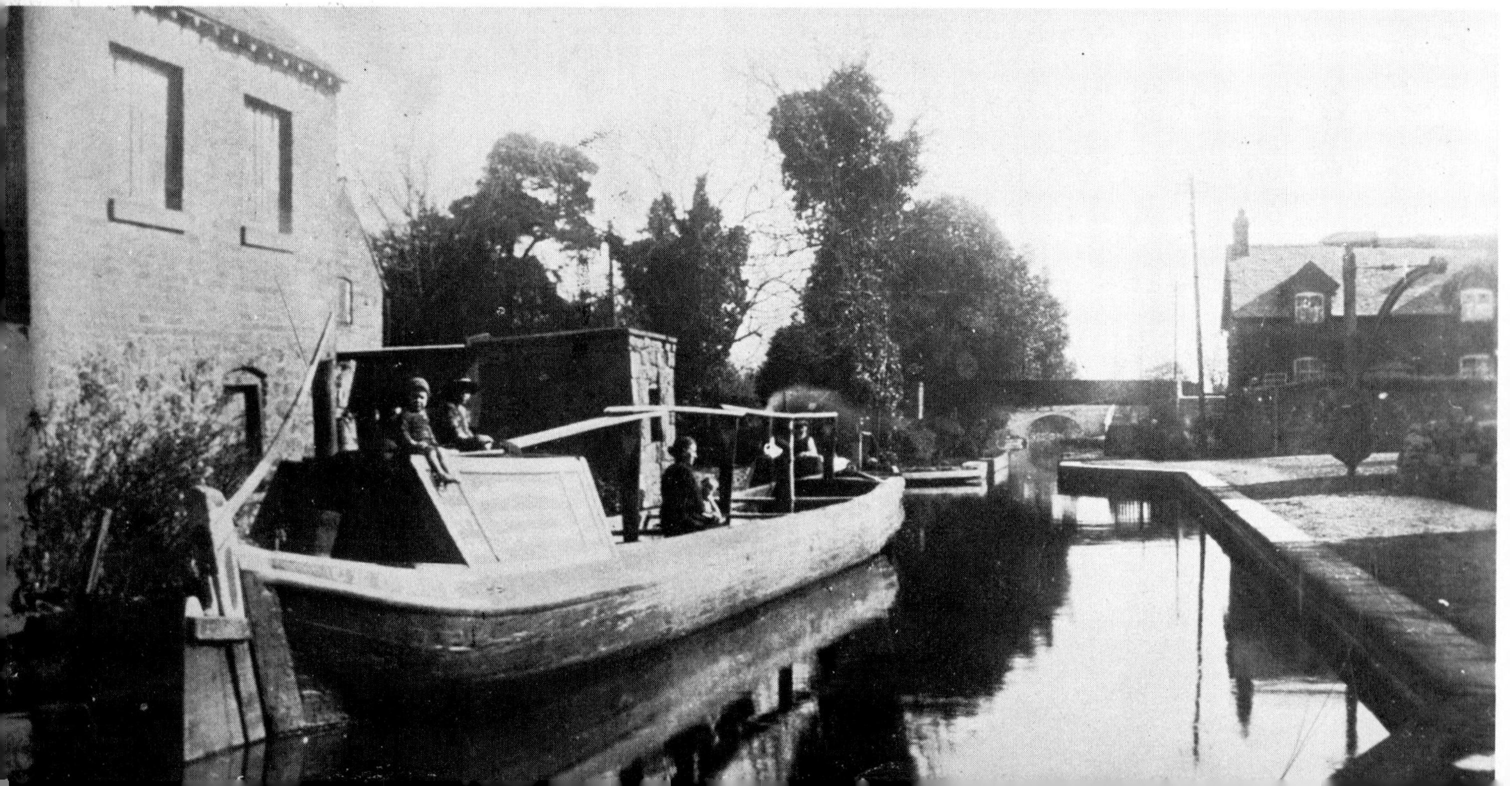

Lifting bridge No. 114 near Buttington, on a picturesque length of the canal between Welshpool and Pool Quay, about 1910.
[J. Elwyn Davies Collection]

Some of the 200 volunteers clear mud and débris during a weekend 'dig' at Welshpool in 1969.
[Harry Arnold]

H.R.H. Prince Charles opens Welshpool Lock on 23 May 1974. With him is Lord Davies of Llandinam, Chairman of the Montgomery Waterway Restoration Group. In 1973, the Prince's Committee adopted seven miles of the canal for restoration with financial aid from the Variety Club of Great Britain.
[Harry Arnold]

The Rogers family (Rogers the Boat), photographed at Welshpool in the 1920's. The boat is the *George,* owned by a local trader. The iron bridge carried the Welshpool and Llanfair Railway over the canal.
[J. Elwyn Davies Collection]

Labour force, 1901; a line-up of men of the S.U.R. & C. Co's Engineering Department during the rebuilding of Severn Street Bridge, Welshpool. [M. R. Welshpool]